A CONTINENT APART

A continent apart

THE UNITED STATES AND CANADA
IN WORLD POLITICS

William T.R. Fox

UNIVERSITY OF TORONTO PRESS
Toronto   Buffalo   London

© University of Toronto Press 1985
Toronto   Buffalo   London
Printed in Canada

ISBN 0-8020-6575-9

Canadian Cataloguing in Publication Data

Fox, William T.R. (William Thornton Rickert), 1912–
A continent apart
(The Bissell lectures; 1982–83)
Includes bibliographical references and index.
ISBN 0-8020-6575-9.
1. Canada – Foreign relations – United States.
2. United States – Foreign relations – Canada.
3. Canada – Foreign relations. 4. United States –
Foreign relations. I. Title. II. Series.
FC249.F69 1985   327.71073   C85-098394-0
F1029.5.U6F69 1985

To A.B.F.

with gratitude for
informed criticism,
empathetic impatience,
and sustained support

Contents

—

Foreword

A Continent Apart is a revised and expanded version of public lectures delivered by the Claude T. Bissell Visiting Professor of Canadian-American Relations in Trinity College, University of Toronto, in 1982–3.

The Bissell professorship was established in 1972 to mark the twenty-fifth anniversary of the Associates of the University of Toronto, an organization of graduates and friends of the university in the United States, with headquarters in New York. It was named in honour of Professor Claude T. Bissell of the Department of English, president of the university from 1958 to 1971 and currently one of Toronto's University Professors. It has brought to Toronto a succession of distinguished scholars, both Canadian and American, and in a number of disciplines. Now lodged in the graduate Centre for International Studies, its responsibilities have been extended to include delivering a number of public lectures, which are published with the assistance of the Associates.

Professor Fox brought high qualifications to the post and has contributed to the published Bissell Lectures a volume which is a worthy successor to John W. Holmes's *Life with Uncle* (1981). Now Bryce Professor Emeritus of the History of International Relations at Columbia University (where he has taught since 1950), Professor Fox has written widely on international relations, and in perhaps his best-known book, published four decades ago, he gave to the English language the term *super-powers*. Professor Fox's interest in Canada's role in world affairs dates from 1945, when, as secretary of the Committee on Enforcement Arrangements at the United Nations Conference on International Organizations in San Francisco, he had an opportunity to observe at close hand and later to write about the effective work of the remarkably able Canadian delegation. But it is as a student of world politics in a much broader sense that Professor Fox was especially welcome to the Bissell professorship and made to it the valuable contribution which is reflected in the present publication. While not ignoring the more parochial aspects of relations across the Canada–United States border, he has brought great learning and understanding to the task of placing that relationship in the context of world politics. He views the relationship of Canada and the United States as a subsystem in the world of states, and his analysis brings a new perspective to the regional analysis of continentalism. His lectures were delivered and his book written before the elections of 4 September 1984 and the ensuing change of government in Ottawa. But as he is concerned with the 'climate' of Canadian-American relations rather than the 'weather,' he has done no more than allude to the latest political developments.

ROBERT SPENCER
Director, Centre for International Studies
University of Toronto

Preface

Twin stars may be very unequal in size and brightness, but they are compelled to revolve around each other as they move through the firmament. The skilled astronomer will know how to measure and predict the perturbations in the behavior of the larger caused by the movements of the smaller, and vice versa. The twin-star analogy may not be perfect for the student of Canadian-American relations who is tracing the orbits of Canada and the United States in the international political skies, but it is suggestive. It is not perfect since Canada and the United States are not rigid bodies held in each other's grip by immutable laws of political gravitation. It is suggestive because Canada and the United States are more than short-hand expressions for describing 25,000,000 people living on one side of a border and 235,000,000 living on the other side.

Enough Canadians feel and are Canadian enough, and enough Americans feel and are American enough, that we may be confident that the twin stars will not collapse into a single star 10 per cent larger than the larger of the North American twins. However, the flow of persons, goods, capital, ideas, cultural influences, personal communications, printed and electronic messages, radio and television signals, etc is much too free and complicated for American-Canadian relations to be dealt with exclusively in Ottawa-Washington terms. States are indeed the most important group actors in modern world politics, but in the pluralistic societies of North America they are by no means the only important class of group actors. In this study of North America (and North Americans) in world politics, care will be taken not to portray Canada and the United States as anthropomorphic monsters with feelings, desires, frustrations, moral characteristics, and calculating behavior of the kind normally imputed to individual human beings.

How the Canadian and American peoples have, acting through their respective national governments, dealt with the housekeeping issues involved in running two huge countries with 4,000 miles of shared and rather open border is a much-studied matter of great and continuing interest, but my focus is not on that important topic. It is on the evolving pattern of American and Canadian relations with the world outside North America. Problems within North America and attendant problems in Canadian-American international relations are important, but in the pages that follow they are treated as context for the present study. As a subsystem in world politics North America has been less studied than many other regions; thus an analysis of what I believe to be an intrinsically important subject may also help to fill a gap in the general study of regional international relations.[1]

That gap has been partly filled by Charles F. Doran's *Forgotten Partnership: U.S.-Canada Relations Today* (Baltimore, 1984). Like *A Continent Apart,* it emphasizes the interconnectedness of direct American-Canadian relations and the two countries' relations with the rest of the world. Our studies are in a sense complementary, for Professor Doran treats their relations with the world outside as context for the study of their relations with each other. His emphasis on 'U.S.-Canada relations today' also complements mine.

A Continent Apart is based on lectures given in 1982–3 and revised before the change of government in Ottawa, the re-election of President Reagan, and what the Toronto *Globe and Mail* described as Prime Minister Brian Mulroney's 'unapologetically pro-U.S. speech' in New York, 10 December 1984. Because this is a book about North America in world politics yesterday and tomorrow as well as today, no substantial revision has been attempted (or seemed desirable) in the light of these important 1984 events.

The focus of these essays makes sense only if one accepts the notion that North America is a region the states of which form a significant subsystem in the world political system or one which for certain limited purposes may be perceived as a bloc actor in the world's political competition. For geopolitical and other reasons, Canadians and Americans, as citizens of the world, find themselves in very similar predicaments. They look over the same North Pole and across the same Arctic Ocean at the same Soviet Union. Both peoples look northeast along the great circle route across the Atlantic that leads to Europe and look northwest across the Pacific toward Asia. Both look south to the clamorous and demanding Third World. That there are opportunities for joint or parallel responses to the threats from or opportunities arising in the outside world is obvious. That the United States and Canada can or ought to respond in all cases in the same way is not. While it is costly for their two governments not to act together whenever it is in the interest of each country to do so, proposals for common policy will remain subject to a double veto as long as the two independent governments make independent judgments of what is in the national interest of their respective countries.

A North American continental perspective such as that revealed in these essays is not, it should be emphasized, a 'continentalist' perspective. One may posit that for certain purposes it is useful to inquire into the 'North American-ness' of North America without taking a position one way or the other as to the kinds of distinctive Canadian policies Canadians should adopt to protect Canada against the danger of having Canadian interests and Canadians' sense of identity submerged and lost sight of. The fears of many Canadians that policies ostensibly in the interest of both countries may turn out to be more American than North American are real and must not be dismissed lightly. They are important to understanding North America's 'foreign' relations.

Three main lines of inquiry will be pursued. Two chapters, the first and the fourth, will explore the utility for Canadians and Americans of envisioning a two-country North America with characteristics that set it apart from the other Americas and from lands on the other side of the two great oceans. Another two, the second and third, will deal with the involvement of states outside North America in North American affairs, resulting from the Old World being summoned to redress the balance of the New, from the New World being summoned to redress the balance of the Old, from intervention by North Americans on their own initiative in the affairs of the rest of the world, or from intervention by states outside North America in the continent's affairs. A third pair of chapters, the fifth and sixth, will consider the range of American and Canadian choice in today's world. The range is described in terms of the necessity, ability, and will of the two peoples and their governments to respond to threats originating in the world outside North America and to exploit the opportunities offered to make that outside world a better one for Canadians and Americans to live with. A brief final chapter summarizes the argument in terms of the forces propelling and the opportunities permitting the two North American governments for certain purposes to work together.

A CONTINENT APART

1 / North America: Two, three, or one?

Canada and the United States are but two of the more than one hundred and fifty states in today's world. In a one-state, one-vote system their votes would not weigh heavily against, say, Africa's fifty-two. In a one-man, one-vote world, the voting strength of Canadians and Americans would also be small. They do occupy one-sixth of the land area of our planet, but there are only a quarter-billion of them; North Americans are only one-sixteenth of the world's four billion people. Yet in this divided world of East-West competition – with the leading powers confronting each other in both Europe and Asia, in both the North Atlantic and the western Pacific, and in the event of a third world war also in the Arctic – the place of the United States and Canada is special.

The schoolchild is taught that something called North America is one of the world's seven continents and that it is a continent in the Western Hemisphere that stretches all the way from the Arctic Ocean south to the Isthmus of Panama. This North America of the schoolchild and of the physical geographer is not a unit of analysis significant for international politics. Like the United States and Canada, every other state in the physical geographer's North America except tiny El Salvador and newly created Belize has both an Atlantic and a Pacific coastline.[1] None but the United States and Canada, however, not even middle-power Mexico, has been active in either of the main theaters of East-West competition, at least since the Second World War.[2] The North America of geopolitics is a North America of the Two.

Expansion to the west was easy in what we are here calling 'geopolitical North America', since the American Indians lacked both the numbers and the technology to halt it. Where the continent was wide the new countries being carved out of the wilderness were bound to be big. There was, however, no historical necessity for it to be divided as it finally was.

The fateful dates in determining the political map of modern geopolitical North America were 1763, 1783, and 1803. Of the three routes into the interior of North America, via the St Lawrence River, the Mississippi River, and Hudson's Bay, before the Seven Years' War the French controlled the first two and the British controlled only the last. The year 1763 saw the British gain control of the St Lawrence; 1783 saw the abandonment by the British of claims to all the territory south of the Great Lakes, thus assuring the new United States of the opportunity to expand over the Appalachian Mountains; and the cession by France of the Louisiana Territory in 1803 not only assured the United States control over the Mississippi gateway into the mid-continent but also opened the way for the Americans to push on to the Pacific. A different outcome in 1763 might have led to a super-power Canada and a middle-power United States.

Such was not to be, and neither Canadians nor Americans need to be told that Canada has only about one-tenth the population and gross national product of the United States. Americans, however, may have to be reminded that in the North America of the Two each is a consequential power in contemporary international politics.

For over forty years, while the United States was being described as a super-power, Canada has been called a middle

4

power.[3] In any scheme for overall measurement of power, a dubious exercise at best, Canada would be ranked among the top dozen or so. For present purposes, however, there is no need to discuss whether number 6 or number 12 (or some number in between) most exactly locates Canada in the world's power hierarchy.[4] Canada *is* number 2 in the power hierarchy of the North America of the Two, but that is not a position of weakness.

Living with inequality is not a new experience for Canadians; 25 million of them live alongside 235 million Americans. In the late eighteenth century the non-Indian population of what is now Canada was under a quarter-million; that of the United States approached 4 million. In 1790, Canada's population was about equal to Connecticut's. By 1850 the population of the United States had grown to 23 million and was slightly larger than that of the United Kingdom. Canada's population did not reach 23 million until the 1970s; it had only about one-tenth the population of its neighbor in 1850, a fraction that has varied little from then until the 1980s.[5] Nevertheless, as the world's wealthiest and most influential state among those in the 20–25-million range, Canada would appear far larger on the world scene if it were located almost anywhere else on the globe than next door to one of the super-powers.

Only on a North American scale, and then only in relation to the United States, could Canada be envisioned as small. Australians are familiar with what one writer called 'the tyranny of distance.'[6] For Canadians the comparable problem might be called the tyranny of proximity. One Canadian prime minister spoke for many of his countrymen when he expressed dissatisfaction with the notion of Canada as a *small* neighbor of the United States. William Lyon Mackenzie King told Parliament in 1944 that 'the simple division of the

5

world between great powers and the rest is unreal and even dangerous.' He added: 'Those countries which have the most to contribute to the maintenance of peace should be the most frequently selected' to be members of what became the Security Council of the United Nations.[7] Few Canadians in the subsequent decades have regarded frequency of election to the Security Council as the authoritative measure of Canada's standing in the world, but few would be any more content than was King for Canada to be grouped with 'all the rest' in the eyes of the world and, in particular, in the eyes of Americans. Status and the constraints of proximity are continuing Canadian concerns; a failure to recognize this fact will lessen the possibilities of effective collaboration between the two North American nations.

Geopolitical North America is a continent apart. Three oceans – the Atlantic, the Pacific, and the Arctic – separate it from the great landmass that Sir Halford Mackinder, the father figure of British geopolitics, called the World Island.[8] The Soviet Union, in contrast, sprawls across the World Island and has powerful countries with which to contend in both its European and its Asian rimlands.[9] North America's separateness has meant different things in successive centuries since the Age of Discovery; the unchanging fact of separateness has interacted with changing conditions in technology, overseas settlement, differential population growth rates, and uneven economic development. Historically, separateness fostered in North America successful independence movements, insular attitudes, and isolationist foreign policies. In the twentieth century the changed conditions have made for the reinvolvement of physically separated North America in the Old World's wars and threats of war.

Classical writers on geopolitics, including Mackinder, have had a Eurocentric view of the world. Mackinder's 'mental map' of the world, to use a phrase borrowed from Alan Henrikson, would have shown North America separated from the European peninsula of the centrally located World Island by what Mackinder called the Midland Ocean and Walter Lippmann the inland sea.[10] The North Atlantic Ocean in geopolitical imagery was thus a kind of oversize English Channel. The nearby insular power, Britain, and the larger one farther away, the United States, plus its less powerful neighbor, Canada, would on such a mental map have a kind of natural unity so as to form what has variously been called 'the Atlantic system' and 'the North Atlantic Triangle.'[11]

In the world of the 1980s, in which Europe is no longer perceived to be so central, two-state North America not only stands apart from the homeland of Europe's traditional great powers, but also stands between the European–North Atlantic and the Asian–western Pacific arenas of major power rivalry. On the other side of the Northern Hemisphere from North America, but directly across the Arctic Ocean from it, sprawls the 8-million-square-mile Soviet Union, located centrally in the Eurasian landmass but like North America between the two main theaters of major-power competition.

The leading powers of the European and Asian rimlands of Eurasia play consequential roles in one or the other of the main theaters of political competition, but none is consequential in both. Thus, Britain, France, Italy, and West Germany are among the leading players in the power rivalries west of Suez, but none of them is still a top-ranking power farther east. Japan and the People's Republic of China,

Indonesia, and India and Pakistan are consequential in eastern, southeastern, and southern Asia respectively but have never been active players in the European theater.

There are exactly three powers able by reason of geography to play consequential roles in both theaters: the two North American states and the Soviet Union. They are the same three that alone would have significant roles to play in the event of a military confrontation in the Arctic. Canada, it should be noted, is not, or at least has not been, as engaged in the Pacific–East Asian arena as in the European-Atlantic. This may well change, since in recent years trade across the Pacific has exceeded that across the Atlantic, long the world's busiest ocean.

Belief in the usefulness of studying the North America of the Two in world politics is based on much more than the geopolitical considerations so far advanced. There are, however, other North Americas in the mind's eye of persons with other concerns and other curiosities. Some of them see a North America of the Three, and some a North America of the One. No one 'mental map' is best for answering every question.[12]

When George III spoke about 'my North American colonies' and the problems of 'that country,'[13] his North America almost certainly excluded the whole western half of the continent but did include, in addition to the thirteen seaboard colonies that were on the verge of making a revolution, Newfoundland, Nova Scotia, what was then called Canada, Bermuda, and the commercially important sugar islands of the Caribbean.[14] A century later Bermuda would still have had a prominent place in the mental map of British leaders' North America. The imperial fortress there, along with the one at Halifax, was critical to Britain's whole maritime strategy and more particularly to the management of her relations with an obstreperous and potentially hostile United States.

Eighteenth- and nineteenth-century Americans often believed that Nature intended what is here called the North America of the Two to be one, and that an enlarged United States should be that one. Three members of the celebrated Adams family found words to express Nature's asserted intention. John Adams proclaimed in 1776 that 'the Unanimous Voice of the Continent is Canada must be ours. Quebec must be taken.' His more radical cousin, Samuel Adams, wrote: 'We shall never be upon a solid footing till Britain cedes to us what Nature designs we should have, or till we wrest it from her.' He proposed to 'cut off a Source of corrupt British Influence, which issuing from there might diffuse Mischief and Poison through the States.'[15] A generation later, John Quincy Adams involved 'the finger of nature' in declaring: 'The world shall be familiarized with the idea of considering our proper dominion to be the continent of North America.'[16]

Twentieth-century students of political geography at the macro-level have also found it convenient to erase the Canadian-American border from their mental maps. Thus, a geopolitical unity has been imputed to 'the United States plus Canada' based on a variety of considerations: the distribution of Canada's population such that each of its geographically separated parts is oriented toward an adjacent part of the United States; Canada's primary products economy, which complements the manufacturing economy of the United States; the dominating position of the United States on the North American continent, with population and gross national product approximately ten times those of Canada's; and Canada's location (on the great circle route between the two super-powers).[17] This last circumstance has meant that the United States cannot act to cope with a Soviet threat without protecting (and perhaps at the same time endangering) Canada too. Only if one had so deterministic a view of titanic struggle between the Soviet and Western camps that it made little difference how many sovereignties there were in North America north of the Rio Grande would the visual image of North America as a single entity seem to make much sense. (It might, of course, make sense polemically for an ardent Canadian nationalist to portray a North America of the One as a self-disconfirming hypothesis: the price Canada is said to be paying for being the tail on an American kite is so great that the rational thing for Canadians to do is to begin flying their own kite.)[18]

For Latin Americans, including Mexicans, 'norteamericanos' refers to persons living north of Mexico, primarily Americans. But J.C.M. Oglesby's depiction of his fellow Canadians as 'Gringos from the Far North' suggests that Latin Americans may not always differentiate between Canadians and Americans.[19] Finally, non-isolationist Americans tend to have a visual image of the United States and Canada as the North America that is active in world politics. They may be attentive to and concerned about such neighborhood problems to the south as the great and only partly controlled flow of Hispanic migrants into the United States, but they do not see such problems as problems in world politics or as problems that especially involve collaboration with Canada.

Americans living near the Mexican border may have a mental map of North America that includes Mexico as well as Canada. This 'southwestern' visual image is shared by political leaders of such differing views as two former governors of California, the Republican Ronald Reagan and the Democrat Edmund G. 'Jerry' Brown jr.[20] The 1983 visit of

Queen Elizabeth II to President Reagan's ranch home in southern California was as much a visit of the queen of Canada as it was one of the queen of England. It was marked by a lunch at which enchiladas and refried beans were served. The lunch was a symbolic affirmation of President Reagan's image of a North America in which Mexico is as close to the United States and Canada as the latter two countries are to each other.

A November 1979 proposal by Reagan, then a presidential candidate, reflected this trilateral image. His call for a 'North American Accord' was a call for a tighter association of Canada and Mexico with the United States. Skeptics, including those who thought of the North America of the Two as a significant grouping in world politics, saw the proposal as reflecting isolationism expanded to incorporate Canada and Mexico. Other skeptics included Canadians already alarmed by the massive American economic and cultural presence in Canada and prepared to object even more vigorously to trilateral continentalism than to the more familiar bilateral version. Still others doubted that Canadians and Mexicans would always want to have Uncle Sam present when they were exchanging views as to how to deal with problems of living alongside a giant. As Canada's ambassador to the United States, Peter Towe, said: 'One of the problems with this hand-holding image is that the person in the middle gets to hold the most hands.' For practical purposes, proposals to give reality to the notion of a North America of the Three have been still-born.[21]

To say that for certain purposes it is useful to envision a two-state North America is not to deny the utility of studying other groupings of states or peoples in which one or both countries may be active. There are many group actors in world politics, and the groups overlap. 'We Canadians,' 'we

11

Americans,' and 'we North Americans' by no means exhaust the list of groupings relevant to understanding the external relations of North America. The North Atlantic Treaty Organization (NATO) identifies one broader grouping in which both countries participate. The semi-annual seven-sided summitry among the leaders of non-Communist advanced industrial states identifies another. Yet another is suggested by the stated objective of the Atlantic Council of the United States, to promote 'mutually advantageous ties between North America, Western Europe, Japan, Australia and New Zealand.'[22] Evidently, the last three are perceived as honorary 'Atlantic' countries. In contrast, ANZUS, the Organization of American States, and the Commonwealth are three in which only one of the North American two is a member. In terms of both security and trade however, Canada and the United States are closer to each other than either is to any other country.

The question of who acts together with whom to achieve common purposes needs to be distinguished from the question of where and with respect to what issues they act together. In the mid- and late 1930s both the United States and Canada were passing from the isolationism of the 1920s to the involvement in European and world affairs of the 1940s. That Canadians, 'our closest neighbors,' dwelled within perimeters Americans would defend was made plain by Franklin D. Roosevelt in two speeches, at Chatauqua, New York, on 14 August 1936, and at Kingston, Ontario, on 18 August 1938. The United States, he declared in his second speech, 'would not stand idly by' if Canada were attacked. Mackenzie King's response two days later was that Canada also had its responsibilities, in particular that of preventing an enemy from attacking the United States by crossing Canadian territory 'either by land, sea, or air.'[23]

As early as 1902 Prime Minister Sir Wilfrid Laurier had observed to Lord Dundonald, the British commander of the Canadian militia, that the militia would not be required for anything but 'suppressing internal disturbances,' since 'the Monroe Doctrine protects us against enemy aggression.'[24] King's response to Roosevelt's Kingston declaration testifies to a change in the relationship from earlier in the century. It was no longer sufficient to describe Canada as enjoying 'a "privileged sanctuary" position ... free to spring to Great Britain's side in any European war ... and secure in the knowledge that, even if by some remote chance Canada itself should be attacked, the United States would step in to repel the invader.'[25] The mutuality of commitment meant that something like a North American security union was in the making.

To form that union, however, more than verbal pronouncements were needed, and another giant step toward making that union a reality came at Ogdensburg, New York, 17 and 18 August 1940. With the fall of France in June 1940 Britain itself was in desperate straits. North Americans felt that the war in Europe had come immeasurably closer. To maintain its lifeline of supply from North America, Britain sought some fifty overage United States destroyers. On its side the United States sought to shore up its position in the western Atlantic by gaining access to offshore bases. Canada's stake in the American-British negotiations was obvious. The fact that they were going on without representatives from Canada present underscored for officials in Ottawa the need to formalize the Canadian-American defense relationship. Accounts differ as to how much Mackenzie King's behind-

13

the-scenes efforts stimulated Roosevelt's sudden decision on 16 August to invite King to meet him at Ogdensburg the next day.[26] Against this background of crisis the prime minister of a Canada at war and the president of a still ostensibly neutral United States met to plan for the joint defense of Canada and the United States, and particularly against an attack on North America by way of Newfoundland, the St Lawrence, or the northeastern coast of Canada. An 18 August joint press statement, variously styled the Ogdensburg agreement or the Ogdensburg declaration, embodied the understanding reached the previous evening that a Permanent Joint Board on Defense (PJBD) would be created 'to consider in the broad sense the defense of the north half of the Western Hemisphere.' It was called 'permanent' to gloss over its being born of crisis, but its creation reflected a permanently changed relation of North America to major conflicts across the ocean. Indeed, Canada's prime minister set off for Ogdensburg without telling the British prime minister; Winston Churchill learned about the board's creation only after the fact.

The board's agenda was in practice limited to formulating plans for Canadian-American collaboration in defending Canada and the sea and air approaches to North America, but the reference to the 'north half of the Western Hemisphere' suggests a wider field for co-operation that later grew very wide indeed. The formula agreed upon at Ogdensburg solved the problem of maintaining in the United States broad support among both isolationists and internationalists for American unneutral neutrality while expanding the form, amount, and geographic extent of American aid in the struggle against the Axis enemies. The Ogdensburg declaration was greeted enthusiastically on all sides in both countries even though public opinion polls in the United States continued until well into 1941 to show overwhelming opposition to the use of American military forces in Europe.[27]

A later publication by the Canadian Wartime Information Board interpreted the Ogdensburg communiqué to mean that 'for all practical intents and purposes Canada had underwritten the Monroe Doctrine' in a 'geographic charter extending across South America to the equator.'[28] In any event, the declaration symbolized a mutual commitment to defend an area larger than the United States and Canada but not so large as to include western Europe.

There was almost certainly calculated ambiguity in defining the limits of 'the north half' of the New World. A popular book of the late 1930s on the defense of the United States was titled *The Ramparts We Watch*.[29] King too had been pushing outward Canada's ramparts to be watched. At the outset of the war in September 1939 he declared that 'the integrity of Newfoundland and Labrador is essential to the security of Canada,' and by the time of the Ogdensburg meeting his government had in effect incorporated Newfoundland into Canada so far as defense was concerned, though it would only later become Canada's tenth province.[30] Ogdensburg opened the way for Americans to stand beside Canadians at the Newfoundland rampart and in defense of the Atlantic approaches to North America. It thus complemented the American negotiations with Britain in the so-called destroyer-base deal.

By defining a quarter-sphere, i.e. the Western Hemisphere down to about the hump of Brazil, as a zone of defense collaboration for the two North American governments, the agreement helped solve Roosevelt's problem of finding a defense posture on which isolationists and advocates of joining the great crusade against Hitler could agree. Isolationists could interpret 'quarter-sphere defense' as expansion of the

15

isolationist base. It also left the wily president free to pursue a practice of which his upright secretary of war, Henry Stimson, disapproved: to engage in 'a quibble over the extent of defense and the limits of the Western Hemisphere' when Stimson thought what was wanted was 'a trumpet call for a battle to save freedom throughout the world.'[31] Roosevelt found even Iceland for purposes of the Atlantic patrol part of the Western Hemisphere. This particular manipulation provided a rationalization for the 'neutral' United States to sink German submarines on sight in a wider area of the western Atlantic. For Canadians and for American internationalist-interventionists Ogdensburg was better than nothing. Further, it had the great merit of not interfering with the first stages of the massive American rearmament then getting under way. For our purposes Ogdensburg demonstrates the reality and significance of the mutually reinforcing capabilities of the United States and Canada in their pursuit of generally compatible but not identical politico-military policies.

One need not accept Mackenzie King's hyperbolic estimate of the agreement at Ogdensburg, that 'in the ultimate importance, it far surpasses the formation of the triple axis.'[32] It did, however, register something enduring and central to North America's place in world politics. The terms *superpower* and *middle power* had not in 1940 been coined; but at Ogdensburg one first sees clearly the super-power United States–middle-power Canada North America of the Two as a distinguishable element in international politics.

We will have occasion later to trace the steps by which the two consequential powers of once-insular North America lost their insularity and were propelled into continuing involvement, some though not all of it joint, in the struggles of the world outside North America. We will also have occasion to consider to what extent common predicament, similar values, and shared heritage have made for joint or parallel choices in foreign policy. We will also want to examine how free either country has been or is likely to be to define the terms on which North Americans participate in the rest of the world's affairs.

2 / From pawns to players

Colonies and trade with colonies were the chief object of the eighteenth-century wars between Britain and France. Ludwig Dehio has described the British Empire of that time as 'an empire in the form of an ellipse with two foci around the rim of the North Atlantic.'[1] The colonies were essential counterweights in the European balance of power, but, continued Dehio, the 'cloven hoof' of the counterweight principle was the migration of power across the sea. Once the continent was settled, its inhabitants were not going to be content to be pawns of some distant government across the sea. One way or another, organized into one state, two states, or many, they would become players.

'The great kings of Europe,' Carl Friedrich has written, 'were in a sense land-hungry farmers.'[2] They treated their European subjects as pawns and would have little reason to treat their New World subjects differently. The colonial subjects may, however, have been harder to control than subjects in Europe if only because they were on the other side of an ocean.

So far as Britain and its North American colonies were concerned, the problem became acute only in the eighteenth century. It was one thing, in the seventeenth century, for the colonists to acknowledge their allegiance to a distant sovereign not in a position to exercise more than a loose control over them. But the eighteenth century saw the hedging about of the power of the English kings, the emergence of mercantilist economic policies, and recurrent Anglo-French wars fought both in and over North America, and it was quite another thing to be made to obey the laws of a British Parliament in which the colonists were not represented and the edicts of a government in London pursuing, in the view of many colonials, British rather than North American interests.[3]

The inevitable occurred as, by very different routes, first the Americans and later the Canadians ceased to be pawns and began to be players in international relations. In the twentieth century the determination not to be, and not to be seen to be, anyone's pawn has been less obvious but not less real in the United States than in Canada. In the days of American unneutral neutrality before Pearl Harbor one could still hear the derisive slogan 'England expects every American to do his duty.'[4] A contemporary equivalent for a Canadian nationalist might be 'Continentalism is treason,' treason presumably because North American policies would be American policies and Canada would revert to pawn status, this time as the pawn of the United States.[5] The old Canadian concern not to be Britain's pawn occasioned a visit to Canada by Lord Hankey, then Sir Maurice Hankey, in December 1934, when Britain's defenses had been allowed to run down and Hitler was beginning to be worrisome. Hankey wanted to know whether England could realistically expect every Canadian to do his or her duty.[6] The South African–born Hankey had for decades been secretary of Britain's Committee of Imperial Defence (CID), a kind of quasi-cabinet in the British government for what would today be called national security affairs and the model for the National Security Council in the United States. The CID's name suggested both empire-wide participation in schemes for empire-wide defense based on decisions made in London and a twentieth-century effort to restore the principle of overseas counterweights for preserving the European balance.[7]

In reference to the Canadian Institute of International Affairs, Hankey made the following startling and revealing diary entry: 'They draw to their ranks extremists of all kinds – "highbrows," isolationists, French Canadians, Irish dissidents with a sprinkling of sound people who for one reason or another – sometimes because they know too much – take no leading part ... The only real "defeatists" I met were leading members of these bodies, and I felt the utmost sympathy for [Prime Minister] Bennett in a tirade he delivered to me against the Institute of International Affairs as a body that did nothing but harm and ought to be abolished.'[8] The new fear that Canada might be used by the Yankees to the south and the old fear that Canada was being used in Britain's imperial defense game reflect a maturing Canadian determination to be nobody's pawn. Hankey concluded that Canada would probably come to Britain's assistance in another war 'if our cause was just, if every effort to maintain peace had been exhausted, and if it was clear to the world that the war had been forced on us.'[9] Canada would decide whether to go to war, how much human and material sacrifice to make, where, when, under whose command, and in what form. Hankey was only recording the long-standing fact that Canada was a North American power and that Ottawa would make its own decisions about war, peace, defense, and peacetime joint Anglo-Canadian military planning. In the 1930s, the answer for both the United States and Canada to any question about cooperative military planning, whether with Britain or with each other, was still no.

If the determination of North Americans to escape from being pawns on an expanded European chessboard was predictable, so were some of the other developments out of which emerged today's North America of the Two. Others, particularly those resulting from technological and demographic change, can be understood after the fact. Still others are genuinely difficult to understand.

Alexis de Tocqueville predicted in the 1830s that Russia and America would one day each sway the destinies of half the globe. It would have been asking too much to have expected him to predict that two North American powers would be among the big seven in the half of the globe not being swayed by the Russians.

It would not have been much of a trick to predict that, although America did not stay discovered very long after Leif Ericsson's visit to Newfoundland, 500 years later, after its rediscovery, America would stay discovered. Economic and political interests would lead to exploitation, settlement, and war to determine in whose interests the various parts of the Americas should be run. It would have been equally easy to predict that in the Age of Discovery the competitors for power in Europe would seek to bring the human and material resources of the newly discovered lands to bear on the central equilibrative process in Europe. A second Europe, it should have been obvious, and was to at least a few people, would be created in any temperate-zone, resource-rich, empty part of the New World. The treasure of the already populated and civilized parts of the New World and the products of its tropical areas not readily available in Europe would, however, initially be more highly valued.[10] Finally, anyone could have predicted a contest for the New World's empty coastal areas and empty inland areas easily reached by water and their exploitation for the fish, forest products, and furs they could contribute to transatlantic trade.[11]

It would have been a little harder to predict (though rather easy to explain after the fact) that the great competitors for New World lands with power based on ships and specie – Spain, Holland, and Portugal – would drop out of the competition. The empty areas across the oceans, it was easy to see after the fact, would be havens for the adventurous, for free-thinkers and religious dissidents, for convicts, and for others whom the European rulers would find it convenient to have relocated in distant parts.

It is similarly easy to see why the second Europe's population and productivity would grow more rapidly than those of the first Europe and that, as the occupied, populated, and more developed parts of this second Europe gained some measure of control over their respective destinies, they would want to expand that control into the adjacent interior and manage the exploitation of adjacent marine resources.

After the fact, one could understand why French-speaking North America, which one might have supposed to be more hostile to British rule than were the thirteen colonies, did not join the American Revolution.[12] One could also understand why thousands of British colonists fled to hospitable or empty nearby areas to make a fresh start, why the independent United States could assure its national security for a century and a half with little peacetime sacrifice for national defense, and why the British North American colonies would later become self-governing without staging a second North American revolution.

But several questions even after the fact seem to me to lack definitive answers. Why did the British triumph in the Seven Years' War create a first British North America that lasted less than a generation? Why in the 'century of peace' after the

22

Peace of Ghent in 1815 did the surviving parts of British North America seem to grow safer from involuntary incorporation into the United States as the British will and capacity weakened to protect them against that eventuality? Why were the disunited, geographically separated, and culturally split colonies to the north of the United States able to tie themselves together politically and with a transcontinental railroad to forge an enduring unity? Why did the second Europe in North America emerge as neither a multi-state subsystem in world politics nor a single vast empire but as a pair of states in a fundamentally stable but very unequal relationship?[13] Why, given the threat that a mighty United States could pose for a sparsely populated and less developed Canada, did Canada not cling more closely to its British connection and respond more affirmatively to British overtures for empire-wide defense planning?

This last question is particularly intriguing, for a different answer by Canada might have confounded Tocqueville's prediction. We might in the 1980s be speaking of a world of the Big Three, a world in which Moscow, London, and Washington were comparable power centers. This is a question to which we shall return in the next chapter.

To begin to understand why the British North America created in 1763 had such a short life one must go back to the beginnings of imperial rivalries in the New World. In the long sweep of history, says Max Savelle, the discovery by Christopher Columbus of the island of Hispaniola in 1492 was an incident in the expansion of Europe.[14] Discovery followed discovery as the outlines of the New World were pricked out and claims were advanced in the name of the particular discoverer's royal sponsor. Spain and Portugal were first in the field and with papal cooperation proposed to be duopolists in the new lands. Britain and France were, however, not far behind and were shortly to colonize much of the Caribbean and seaboard North America and the St Lawrence gateway to North America's interior. The implications of all this did not escape the eye of Richard Hakluyt, the great Oxford geographer, who wrote at the end of the sixteenth century that the English colonies were 'a great bridle' to the power of the Spanish king, for 'if you touche him in the Indies, you touche the apple of his eye... Take away his treasure... [and you will find] his power and strength diminished.'[15]

For two centuries after Hakluyt wrote, colonial North America continued to be an extension of the European chessboard on which Europe's rulers moved their colonial pawns. 'The true balance of power,' declared Choiseul in 1759, 'really resides in commerce and in America.'[16] War in Europe meant war in North America during six Anglo-French wars between 1688 and 1815. Sometimes there was 'war beyond the line' even when there was a respite from fighting in Europe. Thus, the great war for the empire, known in American history textbooks as the French and Indian War, began in 1754, two years before its European counterpart, the Seven Years' War.

From a less august viewpoint than that of the kings of Europe and their advisers what was happening in North America was its settlement by people who were crossing the ocean in search of fish, forest products, furs, fortune, freedom from jail, and a refuge in which to practice a nonconformist faith – in Tom Paine's words, 'an asylum for mankind.' They were people who thought they could do better for themselves in the new Europe than in the old. Some of them, especially in New England, Pennsylvania, and Georgia, thought that they could build a more perfect social order than the one they had left.[17] They were willing to fight for king and country against, say, French and Indians; but they had beliefs, interests, skills, and resources. A king who did not protect them or who violated their beliefs or trampled on their interests might not be able to count on their skills and resources. By 1761 Patrick Henry was declaring that a king who disallowed an obviously salutary act of the Virginia authorities had annulled his compact with the people of Virginia.[18]

These colonists who were building their various 'more perfect social orders' had not been much disposed to cooperate and were in disagreement, sometimes very sharp, over the distribution of western lands. On a largely empty continent they formed, however, a relatively compact area of settlement, hemmed in by the Appalachian Mountains and, to the west, by unfriendly Indians who were often in league with the French. The French and Indian threat promoted a newfound sense of unity among the seaboard colonies. The war that began in 1754 was concentrated in the corridor that led north from New York toward Montreal. That wearying war intensified the colonists' sense of common predicament and common destiny.[19]

By attempting to make a single policy apply wherever possible to all the seaboard colonies (including Nova Scotia) the British may have contributed to the growth of a sense of shared identity. In 1721, for example, London proposed to send out a captain-general who would be responsible for the defense of the 'Empire in America,' i.e. all seaboard colonies from Nova Scotia to South Carolina.[20] More important, policies applied to all colonies called for a response from all colonies, and the resisters to British policy from up and down the seaboard came to know each other.

It is not necessary to trace the earlier process by which the struggle for eastern North America north of Florida narrowed down by the eighteenth century to an Anglo-French rivalry or to describe the long series of wars between Britain and France that together constitute the Second Hundred Years' War. Suffice it to say that for our purposes the decisive struggle was the Seven Years' War. Britain controlled a narrow strip of Atlantic seaboard, but this was a settled, populated, fairly prosperous, and compact area. French control of the two main routes from overseas into the interior, via the St Lawrence River and the Great Lakes and via the Mississippi River and its important tributaries, was frustrating colonial hopes to expand. Overland a Hudson River–Lake Champlain–Richelieu River gap in the mountains opened the way toward Montreal, and the Mohawk gap led via an almost water-level route to the much-desired lands west of the Appalachians.

The adversaries were Britain and France, but colonial interests as well as royal power were at stake. The colonists still remembered, and had bitter memories of, war in the 1740s and the peace treaty signed at Aix-la-Chapelle in 1748. They had sacrificed mightily to capture Louisbourg, then the third most important port on the Atlantic coast, only to see it exchanged at the bargaining table for Madras, which the French had overrun on the other side of the world.[21]

There were voices in London to warn the government policy-makers of the magnitude of the interests at stake in North America. Thus former governor of Massachusetts Thomas Pownall proposed in 1764 that the American colonists be represented in the House of Commons, forming a kind of transatlantic union and reducing the colonists' temptation to form an 'American Union.'[22] During the negotiations that ended the Seven Years' War, Benjamin Franklin, in London, produced two pamphlets arguing that Britain should take Canada rather than Guadeloupe as reward for her military victories, including the one on the Plains of Abraham. That Guadeloupe could have been thought of as an equivalent for Canada almost beggars the imagination, but the 'Canada versus Guadeloupe' controversy produced at least 65 publications between 1759 and 1763.[23]

The end of the Seven Years' War saw the British in control of the whole eastern seaboard of North America and the St Lawrence River gateway into the interior of the continent. Twenty years later the British had lost almost all of the British North America that they possessed before 1762 but kept most of what they had taken from the French!

Victory in 1763 had been won in what was then the most expensive war in Britain's history. There was no question of asking the American colonists to help repay the debts accumulated in nine years of fighting in America, but it seemed reasonable to the British authorities that the colonists should help pay to maintain the peace so dearly bought and so greatly in the colonists' interests.[24]

Some Americans, Franklin among them, had a different view. Thus by 1766 he was asserting that the colonies 'were in perfect peace with both French and Indians' but were entangled in a purely British conflict over Nova Scotia's boundaries and Britain's right to trade with the Indians.[25] However just or unjust this estimate, the Americans did develop in the 1760s and 1770s a sense of grievance that the British authorities could not, or at any rate did not, assuage. Incompetence, lack of information, mistaken zeal, principled inflexibility, and genuine misunderstanding all played their part. The Americans no longer had to fear the French; and if they were kept out of the lands over the mountains, it was because relations between Montreal traders and the Indians in the Ohio territory were fundamentally unchanged by the change of sovereignty in Canada.

27

Proposals to give the colonists representation in Parliament were unsatisfactory: the colonists would have been as much at the mercy of a parliamentary majority as before. Such representation would not have been responsive to the demands generated by the growth of American nationalism. Many colonists saw Parliament as the usurper, for their loyalty was to the king and not to the representatives of those of his subjects who happened to live in Britain. What might have satisfied some colonists, and a few people in England such as Shelburne, was recognition of the American colonies as a separate kingdom sharing a common sovereign with England, a status very like Canada's after 1867. A tax on external commerce to support the navy, which offered protection to mother country and colonies alike, was supportable, but an internal tax not levied by a colonial legislature was not.

The gap in understanding between the London government and the king's colonial subjects was most vividly demonstrated by the Quebec Act of 1774. This act, granting the Québécois religious rights and greatly enlarging Quebec's boundaries, was as unstatesmanlike in offending the aggrieved Americans as it was statesmanlike in ensuring that Quebec would not make common cause with the rebellious colonists. British policy-makers perceived the whole area south of the Great Lakes and north of the Ohio as Montreal's not very valuable hinterland rather than as an area into which the colonists on the narrow eastern seaboard could move as their numbers increased.

The thirteen colonies had such numbers, skills, and wealth that keeping them within the empire was beyond Britain's capabilities. Philadelphia was the second biggest city in the empire, and the leaders of the thirteen colonies had been learning to work together at least since the beginning of the French and Indian War in 1754. They did so ever more effectively as their sense of grievance over the mother country's policies intensified. Britain itself was divided as to the policy to be pursued toward the colonies, and the French were happy to exploit the opportunities colonial rebelliousness offered for the diplomacy of revenge. 'It was,' as Dehio observed, 'the dis-united states of Europe that were the godparents of the United States of America.'[26]

Six years of struggle brought recognition of American independence. Only a few details regarding the revolutionary war and the peace that followed need concern us here. First, the Americans hoped that Quebec might be brought into the new union. The First Continental Congress in October 1774 had denounced the Quebec Act 'for establishing the Roman Catholick Religion in the province of Quebec, abolishing the equitable system of English laws, and erecting a tyranny there, to the great danger, from so great a dissimilarity of Religion, law, and government, of the neighboring British colonies.' In the Declaration of Independence, George III was denounced for 'giving his assent to [various] acts of pretended legislation' including an act 'For abolishing the free system of English laws in a neighboring Province, establishing therein an Arbitrary Government, and enlarging the Boundaries so as to make it at once an example and fit instrument for introducing the same absolute rule into these Colonies.' Not surprisingly, article XI of the Articles of Confederation – accepted by Congress in 1777 and ratified and in force from March 1781 – provided that 'Canada, acceding to this confederation, ...shall be admitted into and entitled to all the advantages of the union ... but no other colony ... unless such admission be agreed to by nine states.' The American overtures, really the overtures of Puritan New England, were spurned by Quebec's leaders.

Second, trade between Quebec and the North American interior and continued access to American markets for British manufacturers were of special concern to the British in the peace negotiations ending the War of the American Revolution. The preamble to the provisional treaty of November 1782 declared: 'Whereas *reciprocal Advantages and mutual convenience are found by Experience to form the only permanent foundation of Peace and Friendship between States;* It is agreed to form the Articles of the Proposed Treaty, on such principles of liberal Equity, and Reciprocity as that partial Advantages (those Seeds of Discord!) being excluded, *such a beneficial and satisfactory Intercourse between the two Countries, may be established, as to promise and secure to both perpetual Peace and Harmony.*'[27]

The two sides were agreed that reconciliation required a reopening of the channels of trade, but the preamble must be read in the light of the boundary provisions of the treaty as finally ratified in 1783. The American negotiators failed in their effort to win the cession of the whole of Canada, perhaps because the French ally believed an undivided North America in American hands to be as inimical to French interests as it had been in British hands.[28] The treaty did push Quebec's southwestern boundaries north from the Ohio River to the Great Lakes, saving what is now Ohio, Indiana, Illinois, Michigan, and Wisconsin for the United States. Jay's Treaty of 1794, however, largely realized one British aim for Canada, to keep trade open with the ceded territories. It provided for 135 years that 'it shall at all times be free to His Majesty's subjects, and to the citizens of the United States, and also to the Indians dwelling on either side of the said [Canadian-American] boundary line, freely to pass and repass by land or inland navigation, into the respective countries of the two parties, on the continent of America.'[29]

30

Third, the bargaining of 1782–3 about the Canadian-American boundary had one result critical to Canada's future. In the final negotiations the Americans offered the British the choice between a boundary along the forty-fifth parallel (from the northern boundary of Vermont and New York to the Mississippi River) and one that follows a rivers-and-lakes route from the intersection of the forty-fifth parallel with the St Lawrence River, through the Great Lakes, along waterways leading from Lake Superior to the Lake of the Woods. Britain chose the second. Had she chosen the first, the territory in which Toronto and all the heavily settled parts of Ontario (except around Ottawa) now lie would have passed to the United States. Canada would have gained territory in parts of what is now Michigan, Wisconsin, and Minnesota, and, if the forty-fifth parallel boundary had been extended to the Pacific, all or most of North Dakota, Montana, and Washington, plus parts of Idaho and Oregon, would have become Canadian. Canada's industrial heartland would have been lost, as would the fertile farmlands of the Ontario peninsula. The United States would no doubt have still turned out to be a super-power, but it is doubtful that the territories north of the alternative border could have coalesced to achieve a middle-power status comparable to that of contemporary Canada.

It took one more struggle to stabilize the new Anglo-American relationship. Although British impressment of American seamen provided the occasion for the War of 1812, trouble in the areas into which Americans were moving and organizing new states exacerbated anti-British feelings. Indian resistance in the Wabash valley of Indiana led by the charismatic Tecumseh, for example, was made possible by Canadian suppliers.[30] Napoleon was making war on Britain in Europe and in the Caribbean, thereby restraining the British from making a major effort to achieve unambiguous victory over their impertinent American cousins. The War of 1812 was a stalemate and Napoleon the de facto ally of the United States in the Battle of Lake Erie and the United States his de facto ally at Waterloo. The balance of power in North America was still intimately related to the balance in Europe.

With peace restored in 1815 by the Treaty of Ghent, Thomas Jefferson, the sage of Monticello, was quick to write to an English friend:

Have you no statesmen who can look forward two or three score years? It is but forty years since the battle of Lexington. One-third of those now living saw that day, when we were but two millions of people, and have lived to see this, when we are ten millions. One-third of those now living, who see us at ten millions, will live another forty years, and see us at forty millions; and looking forward only through such a portion of time as has passed since you and I were scanning Virgil together, (which I believe is near three score years) we shall be seen to have a population of eighty millions, and of not more than double the average density of the present. What may not such a people be worth to England as customers and friends? and what she might not apprehend from such a nation as enemies? Now, what is the price we ask for our friendship? Justice, and the comity usually observed between nation and nation.[31]

Jefferson was not far wrong in his demographic projections.

Since 1815 neither Canada nor the United States has been subjected to serious direct attack from overseas on their continental homelands. A rapidly growing United States was the only conceivable source of direct military threat to Canada until new military technology created the possibility of attack via a polar route from the Soviet Union.

There are times when what does not take place is at least as important as what does. G.K. Chesterton begins his small book on Victorian literature by saying that the most important event in England in the nineteenth century was the revolution that did not happen: the Reform Act of 1832 permitted a peaceful, if not always orderly, emergence of a new order in British politics.[32] Similarly, the great non-event in the British Empire was the Canadian war of independence that never happened. For North Americans the most important was the war with Britain that did not occur as the United States was making good its claim to be a great, indeed a world power.

For Canadian-American relations the miraculous non-event was the annexation that did not occur as the new order within North America was being established. The War of 1812 had ended in a stalemate and a peace based on prudent fortifications and calculations on both sides of the unprofitability of renewed conflict. Costly border fortifications such as those at Quebec did continue to be built for two or three decades, but during the next hundred years the odds steadily decreased that any useful opposition would or could be offered if one day the United States did flex its military muscle. There were wide oscillations in Anglo-American relations, but by any 'enmity-amity' index the trend line of hostility was downward. The myth of the unguarded frontier has long been exploded, notably in a celebrated essay by Charles P. Stacey and in a monograph by Richard A. Preston, who has documented in detail arrangements made to deter and defend against an American invasion of Canada.[33]

Somehow the rough equilibrium between British power in North America and the young republic to the south transformed itself into a stable imbalance between the two continent-wide neighbors in North America, underpinned by increasing recognition of the likely outcome of a military contest between two such unequal neighbors.

In the critical transition period Canada's awkward position as a hostage 'for the benevolent conduct of the British navy toward the United States and the Monroe Doctrine' may have contributed to the safety of the United States, the *future* power of which Britain's leaders may have had reason to fear.[34] For several decades after the War of 1812 peace between Britain and the United States, and therefore peace along the Canadian-American border, depended, in Preston's words, on an 'equilibrium of weakness.'[35] The Americans could take Canada, but the British would then have felt less inhibited about using their naval strength to bombard or threaten to bombard cities on the American east coast. The British could bombard those cities, but the Americans would then be less inhibited in attacking Canada.

During the century between Waterloo and Sarajevo, Britain's relatively small army would have been no more successful than in the 1770s or in 1812–14 in using force on land in North America. Naval power was another matter, and the vulnerability of the American east coast was no doubt a useful constraint on American bellicosity, but it is unlikely that bombardment would have been decisive in any protracted war or brought the Americans to their knees in a short war. Even if it had done so, the long-run cost to Britain of protecting Canada by making a permanent enemy of the United States would have been enormous. Under these circumstances the Canadian connection was a source of danger for Britain rather than of strength; it could have provided the occasion for an Anglo-

American war or even for a more general war also involving enemies in Europe as well as the United States.

That it was not militarily feasible for Britain to defend the North American parts of the empire in the latter part of the nineteenth century is only part of the story. The reigning ideology of free trade and the expectation that at least the settlement colonies would naturally evolve toward independence made any effort to hold Canada in the empire seem hardly worthwhile. The same could be said of a Canada that might be evolving toward voluntary annexation. Only a very rude Uncle Sam could have provoked Britain into accepting war with the United States in order to keep Canada out of American hands.

How then are we to explain the failure of the second British North America, prior to Confederation in 1867, to fall into Yankee hands? One explanation is that the boundary that separates Canada and the United States was, as it still is, quite porous. The frontier was almost no barrier at all in the nineteenth century to the free movement of people, trade, and investment. There were no frustrated Americans to call for annexation so that they might pursue their private interests more freely in the British colonies to the north.

The incorporation of Canadian territory into the United States would have brought no more security to investors in either country than already existed. 'Informal imperialism,' to use a twentieth-century term in a nineteenth-century context, made formal annexation irrelevant. Americans and newly Canadianized ex-Americans could have the fruits of annexation without the United States bearing either its costs or its responsibilities.

Another explanation for the seemingly miraculous failure of the United States to expand north was the widespread perception that in due course 'the ripening fruit' of Canada would fall into the lap of the United States. One member of Congress declared that the 'great Engineer of the Universe has fixed the natural limits of our country.' Another was more precise: 'The Author of Nature has marked our limits on the South by the Gulf of Mexico; and on the north, by the regime of eternal frost.'[36] If indeed the doctrine of Manifest Destiny followed Nature's dictate – that the continent's north, like America's west, should ultimately become part of one vast American empire – there was no need to hurry, no need to provoke a war in order to bring about what was bound to happen anyway.

Nature did not speak with the same urgency that it had in the time of John and Samuel Adams. Manifest Destiny was in fact a little like the Second Coming, a firm but undated expectation. Except for a few impatient millenarians, faithful Christians have been content to wait for that Second Coming. Perhaps the same was true of true believers in America's Manifest Destiny. Even those who might have wished to hurry the process of American expansion might have agreed that the United States was so busy winning the west – with the army, led by officers trained in civil engineering at West Point, busy building bridges and laying out roads as well as chasing Indians – that the problem of expansion to the north would have to be set aside for the time being.

There is yet another line of explanation. There were some people in the United States who did not want to see British North America incorporated into the United States. In the critical decades before the American Civil War there was an uneasy balance between the free states of the North and the slave-holding states of the South. New states to the west were being brought into the union two at a time: one free state and one slave state. Bringing in 'free' Canada might have disturbed the uneasy balance on the survival of which seemed to rest the continuance of the United States as a single country.[37] Of course, if there had been strong sentiment in the North for bringing British North America or some large part of it into the union, a bargain might have been struck. Some Southerners' schemes for expansion into the Caribbean or into still more of Mexico might have been realized. The United States could then have expanded both northward and southward without upsetting the balance between free states and slave states.

Such speculation opens the way to considering still another factor that may have contributed to the failure of Americans to grab Canada while the grabbing was good. North-South disunity was not the only tension that provided Canada with some protection against impulsive Yankee expansionism. Separation of powers in the American system of government meant that expansion, even in the form of voluntary incorporation of territories to the north, could proceed only when the president and both houses of Congress supported the action.

Explanations of non-events can be only speculative, and the non-annexation of Canada is no exception. It is instructive to note what happened when an expansionist secretary of state, William H. Seward, maneuvered to foment annexationist sentiment in Canada. The good feelings between Canadians and Americans symbolized by the Marcy-Elgin trade reciprocity treaty of 1854 were largely dissipated by Canadian failure to prevent hostile Confederate actions along the American-Canadian border and to punish the raiders when they were apprehended. The climax was a Confederate raid on St Alban's, Vermont, in October 1864, following which a Canadian magistrate freed the raiders and allowed them to keep money taken in bank robberies at the time of the raid.

Accordingly, after giving the required one-year notice, the United States denounced the treaty. Reciprocity ended 17 March 1866. Seward and annexationist members of Congress believed that the resulting disruptions of Canadian commerce would help Canadians and especially the Montreal trade and financial interests see the virtue of annexation.[38]

Two other events seemed to be steps toward the fulfillment of Seward's declaration in an 1867 speech in Boston 'that Nature designs that this whole continent, not merely the thirty-six states, shall be, sooner or later, within the magic circle of the American Union.' One was the introduction into Congress, following the most notorious of the Fenian raids, in June 1866 across the Niagara frontier into Canada, of the Taylor Bill; it would have offered any British North American province admission into the Union on request. The other was the American purchase of Alaska negotiated by Seward in 1867 and enthusiastically supported by the chairman of the Senate Committee on Foreign Relations, Charles Sumner, as paving the way for the annexation of Canada.[39]

Whatever Seward's calculations, they turned out to be faulty.[40] The American Civil War and post-war Canadian perceptions of danger from south of the border provided a powerful stimulus toward the formation of present-day Canada. J. Bartlet Brebner has described fear of the United States as 'the principal cause of the germinal federation of four eastern British North American provinces in 1867.'[41] It still seems, however, something of a miracle that British North America, having escaped partial or total annexation, could somehow find its way to Confederation 'from sea to sea to sea.' Seward proved to be a loose cannon that was never quite fired off. The Union army completed its demobilization; and the irritation of the Fenian raids was, if not forgotten, allowed to subside.

The British North America Act of 1867 set the frame for a new nation. The Treaty of Washington in 1871 mended all kinds of fences in relations between the United States and Britain. Only the future could tell how accurate was Lord Carnarvon's prediction that the British Parliament, by passing the BNA Act, was 'laying the foundations of a great State – perhaps which at a future day may even overshadow this country.'[42] The events of 1867 and 1871, however, opened the way for Canada, like the United States, to expand from the Atlantic to the Pacific and for the two countries in their own good time to fill the empty spaces that lay between.

Like Canada and the United States, most of the 150 or so sovereign states in today's world have been carved out of yesterday's colonial empires. The United States may have been the world's 'first new nation' when the thirteen colonies made good the claims they advanced in 1776 in the Declaration of Independence.[43] In the progress from pawn to player, the colonists fought and won, with France's help, a war of independence from Britain, subsequently took full advantage of Anglo-French competition in the New World, and transformed the disunited thirteen colonies into a single united nation. Instead of thirteen pawns there was a new and vigorous player in the game of international politics.

The disintegration of the Spanish empire, the extinction of Quebec's claim to the area south of the Great Lakes (which doubled the size of the new republic), France's cession of the enormous Louisiana territory to the United States (which doubled it again), and the booming growth of American population would have permitted the new republic to play a role outside North America. Not lack of potential to expand its role but the American will to limit it was the determinant.[44] Thomas Paine may have been the first to say that independence could mean separation from Europe's wars.[45] By 1782 John Adams wrote that the Europeans 'will wish to make us a make-weight candle ... We shall be able very often to turn the scale but ... it ought to be our role not to meddle.'[46]

Diplomatic historians may quarrel with Walter Lippmann as to whether the enunciation of the Monroe Doctrine hitched the American wagon to a British star or was a device conceived by President Monroe's secretary of state, John Quincy Adams, to warn the great powers on the other side of the Atlantic, including Britain, that they could go no further in the Americas.[47] Canning said that he called a New World into being to balance the Old. In his proud boast, he may have been a little like Chanticleer claiming credit for the rising sun. Bismarck is reported to have said that the most important fact in modern world politics was that the Americans spoke English. Perhaps he should have said 'most North Americans' rather than 'the Americans.' As it turned out, it was almost a century between the Napoleonic Wars, when the strife of Europe prevented a *decisive* intervention in North American affairs by Britain or any continental European great power, and the First World War, when that strife took a form that fulfilled Canning's prophecy. In that century a new order in North America was established on the basis not of a balance of power but of a stable imbalance.

3 / British Empire and
insular North America

The outlines of a new order in North America very different from the balance of power in Europe, though not wholly insulated from it, were already visible in the 1840s. Annexation of Texas by the United States in 1845, settlement of the Oregon controversy in 1846 by extending the forty-ninth parallel boundary to Puget Sound, and cession of the northern two-fifths of Mexico to the United States in 1848 marked the effective end of British diplomatic efforts to create a regional balance of power in North America.[1] Only if the United States were to break up from within could British North America be made secure from the Yankee threat and American power be contained by normal balance-of-power politics.[2]

Following the Durham report of 1840, self-government was coming gradually to the United Province of Canada and Queen Victoria's other North American colonies. Her subjects in Britain were finding it ever more difficult to discern why they should be called on to defend her subjects in North America, who did not seem willing to take prudent measures to defend themselves and thereby increased the risk for Britain of war with the United States. British leaders hoped that self-government for the colonies would lead them to accept responsibility for self-defense and that Canadians would act effectively to protect themselves.[3] Further, the reigning ideology of free trade made many people of influence in Britain indifferent to the prospect that Canada might be slipping out of the empire toward either independence or voluntary incorporation into the United States. As A.J.P. Taylor wrote about the years after the Second World War, but might equally well have written about the mid-nineteenth century, 'the British did not relinquish their Empire by accident. They ceased to believe in it.'[4]

By the 1870s, the new order in North America was fully established. Union victory in the American Civil War (1865), the British North America Act (1867), the creation of a truly transcontinental Canada by the transfer to federal Canada of British territory east of the Rockies (1808) and the admission of British Columbia (1871), the Treaty of Washington (1871), and the withdrawal (1871) of British garrisons from Canada (except at Halifax) were outward signs of stabilized imbalance in a two-state North American subsystem in world politics.[5]

In this subsystem two huge states almost equal in size but unequal in almost every other respect occupied the fertile, well-watered, resource-rich, and (by European and Asian standards) rather empty northern four-fifths of North America. Throughout history large states on the periphery of a cluster of intermittently warring states have been able to grow unchecked by states centrally located in the cluster, each of which must guard itself against its neighbors. Macedonia to the north of the Greek city-states, Rome on the western edge of the Hellenic world, France just over the Alps from the city-states of the north Italian plain, and Britain across the channel from continental Europe's warring states – each in its turn grew in size and strength while its neighbors fought each other.

History does not repeat itself mechanically, and in the second half of the nineteenth century relatively unconstrained growth was occurring at both the eastern and western edges of the European state system's major arena of confrontation. Further, unconstrained growth at the western edge of the system, in North America, was not just of one state but of two.

The hasty demobilization of the million-man Union army in 1865 suggests that the threat of conquest of what is today Canada or of any major part of it was slight, and the Treaty of Washington (1871) greatly reduced the chance that Canada might be dragged into an Anglo-American war not of its making. Britain was not going to defend Canada.[6] In spite of the expansionist aspirations of men such as William H. Seward, none who favored annexation, whether Americans or Canadians, advocated the use of force.

The next three or four decades were to see a remarkable evolution in Anglo-American relations, variously described as the rise of Anglo-American friendship and the decline of Anglo-American hostility.[7] They were also to show whether Canada, left alone beside its giant neighbor, would become a truly independent player in international politics or, alternatively, would cease being a pawn of Mother England only to become one of Uncle Sam.[8] If the former were the case, these same decades would show the extent to which Canada would use its independence in a way that demonstrated its 'North American-ness' and the extent to which it would use it as a supporting player in the emerging empire-Commonwealth.

The world was not standing still while the new order in North America was being consolidated. Bismarck's dazzling successes in three short wars, especially his humiliation of

France in 1871 (the year of the Treaty of Washington and the recall of the garrisons from Canada), were making British policy-makers concerned that Germany, replacing Russia as the *bête noire* of British diplomacy, might attempt to overturn the European balance. The new German threat turned a reluctant Britain's attention back toward Europe and came from a country that, unlike France, Russia, and the United States, had previously posed no threat to any part of Britain's world-girdling empire. Perhaps the worst nightmare of Britain's leaders after 1871 was that in an Anglo-German war the United States might enter on the German side.[9]

Whether because of that fear or of a sense that the American cousins might be needed in an hour of peril or a combination of the two, the British mended their fences with the United States, especially after 1895. In the process, as Lionel Gelber demonstrated in the 1930s, they did not always put Canada's interests ahead of Britain's.[10] With the French and eventually also the Russians they mended their fences by joining in the Entente Cordiale. And in 1902 they made an alliance with Japan which was to disturb Canadians as they became aware of potential trouble between the United States and Japan. So far as Canada itself was concerned, the British moved from being unwilling providers of garrisons to being active searchers for a formula by which the old mistress of the seas could get some help from the richest and most populous of her self-governing colonies. Canada meanwhile moved from reliance on Britain for protection against the United States to reliance on the United States for protection against every power but its American guarantor.[11] How little Canadians needed protection from the United States in the last decades of the century is shown by the use the Americans made of the forts on their side of Lake Ontario. They used them to billet soldiers brought back from Indian-fighting for rest and recreation.[12]

As Britain was turning outward – making alliances, mending fences, and asking its self-governing colonies both to look to their own defense and to contribute to the defense of the empire – Canada was turning inward. Pressure on Canada after Confederation to pay its imperial defense dues was no more successful than had been pressure on the thirteen American colonies before 1776. The pressure and proposals for empire-wide defense arrangements sharpened for Canadians the choice between imperial federation and independence, perhaps in the form of loose association with Britain under a common sovereign. (There was a third choice, merger with the United States; after Confederation it could have occurred only on Canadian initiative or as a consequence of an Anglo-American war in which Canada was used as a base for military operations against the United States.)

Imperial federation would have permitted a unified naval strategy, but for Canadians there were at least three difficulties. First, no credible scheme was ever advanced for giving the part of the empire most directly concerned with a particular decision a commensurate weight in making that decision; it was easier to think of ways of sharing the burden than of sharing the decision-making. Second, Canada was largely inaccessible to defense by the Royal Navy, particularly as the United States moved to improve its coast artillery and construct a coastal defense navy; imperial federation would have solved no Canadian defense problems.[13] Third, a large Canadian army, the most obvious use of which would have been to support Britain in a war with the United States, would have been so viewed in the United States and thus a source of

45

danger for Canada, something that Sir John A. Macdonald did not fail to note.

At the 1897 colonial conference in London, Canada's prime minister, Sir Wilfrid Laurier, responded to Britain's overtures for a substantial Canadian contribution to colonial defense by saying: 'If you want us to help you, call us to your council.' In the official photograph of that conference the colonial secretary, Joseph Chamberlain, sat while the first ministers stood; it was not yet a time for councils among equals.[14] By 1902, when the next such conference was held, Chamberlain had evidently begun to learn that the colonial children had to be treated as adults if they were to be persuaded to contribute to the support of an aging parent. He spoke gratefully of the empire's voluntary help in the prosecution of the war in South Africa but said that any proposals for 'a more definite and closer union' of Britain and the self-governing colonies must come from the latter. He spoke of Britain as 'the weary Titan' staggering 'under the too vast orb of its fate' and asserted that when the self-governing colonies were prepared to share in the burden of empire, 'we shall hasten gladly to call you to our councils.' There was no positive response from the overseas leaders. Laurier, whose government was spending on defense one-fifteenth per capita of what Britain was spending, was politely noncommittal.[15] Wary Canada in effect said 'no' to the weary Titan.

The system of defense cooperation that was to evolve and that provided Britain with heroic support in two world wars was, as Richard Preston has pointed out, an invention of the colonies-turned-dominions and not based on any proposals coming from London. Parallel action in association, not integration or federation or any form of elaborate institution-building, opened the floodgates of sacrifice from overseas in Britain's hour of need.[16]

Canada was by far the biggest prize to be won over to the notion of empire-wide foreign and military policies. The Australians, the New Zealanders, and, in the years after the Peace of Vereeniging ending the Boer War (1902), the South Africans were probably more disposed than the Canadians to look with favor upon a scheme of imperial federation. It is perhaps doubtful that an arrangement could have been made to satisfy both Britain and the dominions, but the failure to develop such a system was fateful to Britain's loss of any chance of being the center of a third, Commonwealth superpower after 1945. And Laurier effectively vetoed such an arrangement.

Laurier wanted government-to-government talks, not colonial prime ministers chatting en masse every few years with the colonial secretary and attending occasional staged sessions of Britain's Committee of Imperial Defence. He wanted bilateral negotiations between Britain and Canada at the time of actual crisis rather than blank checks signed in advance, with the amounts of troops, ships, arms, dollars, etc to be filled in later. He did not want Canada committed to execute decisions in which its government might not concur. His Conservative successor, Sir Robert Borden, may have been more willing than any Liberal prime minister to be called to London's councils; unlike Laurier, he did not have to maintain Quebec's support to stay in power. Borden's experience before and during the First World War, however, convinced him that London could not make the emerging Commonwealth produce a strong and supple common defense policy. Without that there was no way to make the post-1945 world tripolar rather than bipolar.

Canadians' sentimental and political ties were to Mother England, not to a congeries of possessions on which the sun never set. The sturdy editor of the Winnipeg *Free Press*, John

47

W. Dafoe, condemned imperial federation as a scheme of British imperialists to undermine Canada's control over its own foreign policy. Canadians, he declared, had no interest in Britain's 'thousands of petty quarrels ... along the borders of her vast empire'; but he professed a willingness to see Canada aid Britain if necessary in a time of crisis.[17] O.D. Skelton, professor-turned-External-Affairs-bureaucrat and 'guardian of Canada's isolation' in the Mackenzie King era, could detect 'no community of interest between Canada and Australia and Timbuctoo, or whatever other part of the map a Jingoistic spree may chance to paint red.'[18] In writing about the making of a new international order after 1945 John Holmes declared that 'the utter impracticality of the idea of a common policy [for the dominions] ought to have been evident,' and there was a great deal of Canadian history to substantiate his statement.[19]

Canada's pre-1914 position as to its imperial obligations and its post-1919 attitude toward obligations under the Covenant of the League of Nations were similar and uncomplicated. There was to be no involvement without representation and without veto power in decisions involving the possible use of Canadian forces, and very little even then; no involvement in secondary wars in remote parts of the world; and no commitment to fight in a major war until a crisis occurred, and then only when Canada's involvement would make a difference and if its forces were to be kept separate and commanded by its own officers. Even Prime Minister R.B. Bennett was no more willing than Laurier, Borden, or King to accept membership or even observer status in the Committee of Imperial Defence.[20] Until 1939 'no prior commitment' was as firm a position in Canada as it was in the United States. Echoes of this position were heard in the debate at the San Francisco Conference in 1945 over the provisions of chapter VII of the Charter of the United Nations relating to enforcement arrangements.[21]

In both the United States and Canada between the two world wars isolationism and internationalism were twin faces of the same basic North American position: North Americans would not commit themselves in advance to participate in Europe's 'unclean' power politics. In an extreme case they might join in a crusade to transform a system in which evil warmakers had again plunged helpless peoples into senseless slaughter, but it was politically dangerous, at least in the United States, to admit that the contingency might arise.

Canada's ability to say 'no,' like that of the United States, was firmly established, as were its ability and willingness in the exceptional case to say 'yes' and then contribute hugely to the prosecution of a war into which the country had freely entered. This position established Canada in the eyes of the world as a consequential international player in its own right. At the Paris Peace Conference in 1919 the Canadian delegates had hoped to have the provision in article 10 of the League Covenant providing for an alliance of all against any aggressor anywhere deleted or weakened. Their effort failed, but after Canada had joined the league, Canadians at Geneva worked to water down the article 10 commitment. They did so for many of the same reasons that opponents of the league in the American Senate voted to keep their country out of the league altogether. To Canada membership in the League of Nations gave greater freedom of choice because it provided an additional forum in which Canadian policy could be spelled out publicly and independently of both Britain and the United States. Equally important, Canada's membership reiterated to the world and to Canadians themselves that their country had found its voice and would in all things speak for itself.

Canadians were as free, so far as the Americans were concerned, to choose the path of neutrality or the path of war as were the Americans themselves. Only in the unthinkable case of a Canadian government entering into an alliance with a power that might plausibly get itself into a war with the United States could one have envisioned firm American pressure on Canada to desist.

By the early 1920s Canadians had been demonstrating that they did not mean for Canada, as the North American part of the empire, to allow Britain to speak for it. Loring Christie, Prime Minister Arthur Meighen's closest adviser on foreign affairs, as he had been Sir Robert Borden's, declared that 'in matters of high policy respecting North America the voice of Canada should be predominant as far as the British Empire is concerned.' The Canadian position was, said Meighen, that with respect to any matter of the 'Empire's foreign policy in which any Dominion is peculiarly concerned, the view of that Dominion must be given a weight commensurate with the importance of the decision to that Dominion.' The reference, he said, was to 'our relations with the United States.'[22] Made in 1921, it had particular application to a proposed renewal of the Anglo-Japanese alliance.

Canada became increasingly dissatisfied with the alliance as Japan began to challenge American paramountcy in the Pacific, and its uneasiness was crucial in British calculations leading to the termination of the alliance as part of the complex package of agreements concluded at the Washington Conference on Naval Disarmament in 1921–2. The Canadian position prevailed against the opposition of Lord Curzon, the Committee of Imperial Defence, Britain's senior military leaders, and the governments of Australia, New Zealand, South Africa, and India.[23] This is evidence both of the status of independent player in world politics that Canada had already achieved and of its government's zeal not to be seeming to make common cause with a potential enemy of the United States. However, American failure to invite Canada to the Washington conference, in the outcome of which Canadians had an enormous stake, suggests that the Americans still thought of Britain as able to speak for the whole empire.

As the less powerful of the North American two, Canada has had very great, though not unlimited, freedom of choice on the great questions of war versus peace, of alliance commitment versus isolation, and since 1945 of high versus not-so-high peacetime defense budgets.[24] American military strength and power potential are part of the protective context in which Canada makes critical decisions as a sovereign state, but that strength is not available to coerce Canadian decisions in these matters. It is even less available for intimidating Canadian decision-makers dealing with questions unrelated to international peace or North American security.

Canada was basically isolationist before 1939. It was unlikely that political-military activities outside North America would embroil its relations with the United States. Canadians, however, seem to have been quite free from American pressure in deciding how far they would become involved in imperial defense schemes or in colonial wars. The extent of Canadian participation in the Boer War, for example, was not decided with one eye fastened on Washington. Neither was the question of the conscription of Québécois in either world war, to say nothing of Canada's prior decisions to go to war, which in both wars occurred long before any politician in the United States dared even hint at advocating American entry.

51

The great events at Kingston in 1938 and at Ogdensburg in 1940 only made explicit what had been implicit. Canada could play, if it chose, an active role on the world stage and at the same time remain under the sheltering canopy of American power, which in the period of American neutrality was still very largely naval. No enemy of Canada could attack it, its war industries, and its vast military training facilities, while its soldiers were off fighting and its people were accomplishing near-miracles in war production, without having to make war on the United States too.

How is one to account for a stably unbalanced international order in North America, one so markedly different from that of balance-of-power Europe? In the second half of the nineteenth century the Atlantic Ocean insulated North America from compulsory involvement in the politics of the European balancing system. The growing population and industrial power of the United States would have made its defeat in a long war a formidable and probably impossible task, and there was no chance whatever of its defeat in a short war. Britain's role was dual. On the one hand, its dominance in the Ocean World of the nineteenth century protected North America against effective intervention in North American affairs by any continental European power. On the other hand, Britain's growing need to protect itself against a threatened upset of the balance of power on the European continent, together with its declining ability to shape the course of events in North America, explains the imbalance in North America but does not explain its stability. In particular, it does not explain the creation and survival of a Canada that is not just a satellite of the United States.

The simplistic view of sovereign states each driven in a dog-eat-dog world to maximize its power position has a certain analytical utility when applied to competition among the great powers in the multipolar European system of the seventeenth to twentieth centuries. It is less useful in explaining the relations of Canada and the United States with each other or of the two of them with the rest of the world. The 'North American-ness' of the United States and Canada, to be discussed in the next chapter, is partly explained by separateness from Europe during the formative periods of American and Canadian history. Nineteenth-century technology and international politics made that separateness more significant then than it was to be later. Distinctive North American ways of thinking about and responding to problems posed by the world outside were almost bound to reveal themselves. Today the Atlantic no longer seems so wide and its width has diminished relevance for the New World's ability to remain aloof from the strife of the Old.

Insularity once offered North Americans freedom from constant preoccupation with the physical security of their homeland. A favorable population-resource ratio meant that 'the peace dividend' – the wealth available for public or private expenditure because it did not have to be spent on defense – could be very large. In the longer term some of the peace dividend could be (and was) converted into accelerated growth.[25]

We have spoken of the insularity of North America in the past tense. The two world wars suggest that the only choice North Americans have had in a protracted general war, once it had begun, was when to enter. Canadians chose in both wars to enter early. The Americans chose in both to wait until war was thrust upon them. Both nations had chosen in the years before 1914 and before 1939 to pursue isolationist paths and to make no important contributions to deterring a threatened conflagration. Isolationist perspectives prevailed, sometimes in high places, for many years after insularity was lost.

Progressively, and a generation before it happened to the same extent in North America, Britain was drawn back into the strife of the continental European powers. In 1919, Sir Halford Mackinder described this breakdown of a self-maintaining balance of power in terms of a struggle between land power and sea power, one, he might have said, between the Russian Behemoth and the British Leviathan. Like other Britons he eventually came to see Germany as a greater threat than Russia.[26]

The North American prophet of geopolitics, Nicholas Spykman, started from a different point. He assumed, during the years before the United States entered the Second World War, that Britain was fully engaged in stopping an aspirant to hegemony in Europe and that Britain's effort might prove insufficient. This was not an implausible assumption for someone writing after the fall of France in June 1940. Spykman adopted an isolationist stance for the purposes of his argument and asked whether, if some leading power were to gain hegemony in Europe, North America would be able to defend itself against an aggressor that could bring the whole strength of the Old World to bear upon the New. He concluded that the New World would lose in such a struggle and that, to forestall that disaster, the rimland areas of Europe and Asia, meaning at least western Europe and Japan, must not be allowed to come under the control of a hegemonic Old World power.[27] Even a hard-core isolationist would not know how to rebut this argument for abandoning a set of go-it-alone attitudes. Spykman's eye was on Washington, not Ottawa, but the implications of his analysis were something for both Americans and Canadians to ponder.[28]

One more development remains to be noted in connection with North America's security in the 'post-insular' era. It was the prospect, indeed almost the certainty, that irretrievably decisive events in a future general war would occur long before men and weapons not ready at the start of the war could be thrown into the battle. Moreover, in a deepening crisis, when questions of war and peace hung in the balance, men not yet mobilized and trained and weapons not yet produced could have no deterrent power.

The two North American states could not in a future war do what Canada did in the Second World War, wait until the war had occurred before deciding how it would behave, or do what the United States did, wait until it was pushed into war before joining the nearly exhausted Western democracies. The Canadian government had long said that it would decide 'when the time comes.' By 1943 its position was shifting. Louis St-Laurent, anticipating the important role he was to play later in the making of the North Atlantic Alliance, said to Parliament that there would be 'greater safety in an association of democratic and peace-loving states willing to accept more specific international obligations.'[29] After 1945, when lead-times became long and big wars could be very short, one had to plan in time of peace, long before the outbreak of war.

A world war, Washington and Ottawa came to believe, could not be deterred or effectively waged without peacetime preparedness, including coalition war planning, and North America could not be defended except by deterring or defeating any large-scale attack on either western Europe or North America. In the eighteenth century the thirteen colonies needed protection from Europe – from the French before 1763, from the British after 1776. In the nineteenth century Canada first sought protection from and then expected protection by the United States. In the twentieth century the role reversal between Europe and North America has been completed: western Europeans need protection that only North Americans can offer, protection that, for their own good reasons, they continue to provide.

4 / The North American-ness
of North America

In previous chapters we have considered the geopolitical aspects of the North America of the Two, noting the advantages of insularity now lost and the new roles in world politics played by the two countries. These new roles were created, as we have seen, in response to changing technology and the two nations' rate of growth in wealth and power, so much more rapid than that of Britain and the continental European powers. Location and growth rates, however, are not factors that operate in a vacuum. The American and Canadian political systems in the 1930s produced as leaders Franklin Roosevelt and William Lyon Mackenzie King, not Adolf Hitler and Karl von Schuschnigg. A United States headed by a Hitler would have swallowed up a Canada headed by a Schuschnigg, and North America's subsequent role in world politics would have been vastly different.

One tension in the search of North Americans for their sense of identity has been between feeling different from 'Europe,' meaning continental Europe and its periodic general wars, and feeling different from England. English political institutions underwent a sea change in crossing the Atlantic and have been following a separate line of development for several generations.[1] Is it the English Channel or the Atlantic Ocean that marks the eastern limit of an area of shared values, institutions, and attitudes? The answer, of course, has historically been both, though Britain's entry into the European Economic Community makes Britain appear more European than at any previous time.

'Anglo-Atlanticity' has led, as A.R.M. Lower has pointed out, to dreams of the American Revolution being reduced to a 'mere incident.'[2] The most brilliant flowering of the special relationship in which Britain too, not just Canada, was seen as 'independent but not foreign' was during the Second World War.[3] J. Bartlet Brebner's *North Atlantic Triangle* was produced in 1945, as the last of twenty-five volumes on Canadian-American relations.

For Canadians there was another tension in their search for identity, but it was three-way – not being European, not being British, and not being American. Canada, one member of Parliament is reported to have said, was founded on anti-Americanism and needs to go on an anti-American binge at least once every five years.[4] In any effort to describe the North American-ness of North Americans we need not, however, concern ourselves with whether the similarities or the differences are more striking. Both are important to understanding the roles played by the United States and Canada in the international politics of our time.

One shared Canadian and American characteristic – a national self-image of great moral worth – may have seventeenth- and eighteenth-century roots. Ezra Stiles, then president of Yale University, in a 1783 sermon, 'The United States Elevated to Glory and Honor,' spoke of his country as God's 'American Israel.'[5] The implication was that the Atlantic Ocean was an oversize Red Sea and North America the modern promised land. Stiles might better have spoken of a North American Israel.[6] Woodrow Wilson was echoing Stiles when he spoke of 'the full freedom of a virgin world.'[7] Expansion by conquest may be depraved, but expansion into a virgin world is not. The notion, however, that 'political gravitation' would bring the less populous North American democracy into the embrace of its great neighbor seems to have died some time between 1890 and 1920. Charles Vincent Massey declared that the idea of political union now 'belongs to the sphere of the antiquarian or the humorist.' President Warren G. Harding, in his 1923 speech in Vancouver, made perhaps the final oblique official reference to annexation when he said: 'Let us go our own gaits along parallel roads, you helping us and we helping you.'[8]

The two countries have gone 'along parallel roads' to poor old western Europe's aid by joining in two world wars, by their North Atlantic Treaty commitments, by their subsequent participation in coalition military planning, and by deployment of American and Canadian forces and weapons in western Europe, the North Atlantic, and the Mediterranean. They have done so because enlightened selfishness requires that they be concerned with the security of the whole Western world. Like most leaders in most countries they assert a perfect congruence between enlightened national self-interest and the interest of the wider international community. Politicians almost never say: 'Policy X, though bad for my country, is so good for the international community that we will adopt it.' Neither do they say: 'Policy Y, though bad for the international community, is so good for my country that it is our policy.' There will be a gap between words and action in both countries. American public oratory is likely to be a little more grandiose than the Canadian, but that does not get us very far in the search for the distinctive American, Canadian, and North American values and behavior in foreign policy.

Claude Bissell tells us that Walt Whitman is more popular in Australia than in Canada, that Australians and Americans have made folk heroes of their bushrangers and their high-waymen, their Ned Kellys and their Jesse Jameses, but that the Canadian heroes have historically been the Royal Canadian Mounted Police, the Mounties, 'who always got their man.'[9] Seymour Lipset cites this comment by Bissell in his comparison of the United States, Britain, Australia, and Canada; he finds that while English-Canadian society is less egalitarian than Australian or American it stands midway between British and American societies in egalitarianism and with respect to four other variables. He suggests that cultural differences between Canada and the United States may be related to the revolutionary tradition in one country and a counterrevolutionary experience in the other, to the greater importance of achievement-oriented nonconformist Protestants in the formative period of American culture, and to the very different way the American west and the Canadian west developed. His starting-point is a statement that 'from the comparative perspective of world-wide cultural variables, there can be little doubt that these four nations represent different regional versions of one culture.'[10]

Americans, it is said, tend to discover similarities between Canadians and Americans while Canadians tend to discover differences. This may reflect only a normal bias of scholars, to be readier to discover what they want to discover than the opposite.[11] Canada's scholars may, not always consciously, be trying to satisfy a need of Canadians to affirm their identity, and American scholars may be exhibiting a form of cultural imperialism. The difference between the two groups of scholars may reflect real differences between the two societies, one of which is greater Canadian sensitivity to that distinctiveness. Canadian policy-makers tend not to follow an American lead without careful examination and full discussion.

Canadians' more developed sensitivity to differences and their efforts to preserve them no doubt help maintain the stability of the stable imbalance in North American international relations. So perhaps does the Americans' insensitivity in a benignly perverse way, for the sometimes-irritating American attitude that Canadians are 'basically just like us' reinforces the notion that it ought to be possible to settle problems between the two countries by reference to shared values. Hence it would be inappropriate to use American muscle to constrain Canadian policy choices.

However much Americans may overstate and Canadians understate the community of values, attitudes, social practices, common heritage, trading opportunities, and security interests, Lipset was surely correct in his assumption that we are dealing with 'different regional versions of one culture.' The renowned Canadian diplomat Hume Wrong has described his country as 'a North American democracy fighting for North American issues and values.'[12] He was not the only informed Canadian who has found that at least some perspectives about the methods and ends of foreign policy are shared by the two countries' policy-makers. Prime Minister Trudeau declared that his country's foreign policy ought to reflect the attitudes of a caring, compassionate people who believe in social justice.[13] Every Canadian prime minister and every American president should be able to subscribe to such a statement, but being caring and compassionate and believing in social justice are not a North American monopoly.

Trudeau's statement has operational significance for wealthy, stable democracies wherever they exist. Canada and the United States have a special opportunity to be virtuous that comes from their North American location. Their historic insularity generally discouraged, and diminished the effectiveness of, European intervention in their affairs. It encouraged a philosophy of choice in foreign affairs that contrasted sharply with continental European doctrines of necessity.[14] It gave the United States and Canada, as it did Britain until late in the nineteenth century, wide choice as to how to relate to the outside world, particularly as to the timing and extent of intervention in Europe's affairs.

Physical separation from Europe and the certain prospect of rapid future growth created an unusual opportunity for choice. Widely held views about the supposedly sordid power politics of Europe helped define the task of making a fresh start across the Atlantic. Negative views about Europe have a long history in both countries. John Adams took no exception to Baron von Noltke's hope that Americans would 'have sense enough to see us in Europe cut each other's throats with a philosophical tranquillity.'[15] A tendency toward immobilism and inaction prompted by suspicion of European power politics was reinforced in Canada by 'the French fact,' that one of Canada's two founding peoples would be unenthusiastic about following a British lead in European and imperial politics. In the American case it was reinforced by the separation of powers in the federal government, which greatly complicated presidential initiative.

The United States, said Lipset, was the first 'new nation,' but by now it is a rather overage new nation. Canada is older than a great majority of the member states of the United Nations. What makes the two countries special is that their new-nation psychological heritage – the image of good America in contrast to bad Europe – is combined with the psychological heritage of insularity and the availability of human and material resources applicable to the implementing of high-minded foreign policy pronouncements.

Let us look further at the 'fresh start' 'good America, bad Europe' set of perspectives. Canadians and Americans established, decades before western Europe, what Stanley Hoffman calls a 'zone of peace' and Karl Deutsch a 'security community.' Their success opened the way for a spate of self-congratulatory rhetoric, particularly in the years just before 1914 when plans were being made to celebrate 'a Century of Peace' on both sides of the Canadian-American border.[16] With the role in world politics of the old great powers of western Europe greatly diminished from its pre-1939 dimensions, Europe-bashing no longer seems worth the trouble; but one of the traditional ways of asserting North American virtue used to be to make unfavorable references to Europe as a whole, and sometimes to Britain in particular.

James Eayrs begins the first volume of his magisterial series *In Defence of Canada* by demonstrating how many leaders of new nations have claimed that in their conduct of foreign relations they have been liberated from the evil attitudes and sordid practices of traditional diplomacy. Thomas Jefferson, for example, described diplomacy as the workshop in which Europe's wars were manufactured. A Canadian delegate at Geneva wrote in 1920: 'It was European policy, European statesmanship, European dislike that drenched this world in blood.' One of Mackenzie King's correspondents in 1923 wrote about 'the war-drunk lunatics of Europe ... *one and all cannot be trusted.*' King's intimate adviser, O.D. Skelton, put the accent on North American-ness rather than on North American virtue when he wrote at the time of Locarno: 'Britain is part of Europe and Canada is separated by three thousand miles of sea and incalculable differences in culture, in problems and in outlook. We are British North America; Britain is British Western Europe.'[17] Where the

French Canadians fitted into the Skelton formulation is not clear, but they presumably would have been still more unlike the British 'in culture, in problems and in outlook' than the English Canadians.

Canada's search for identity led Canadians to stress their North American-ness when they sought to differentiate themselves and their policy from the British and Britain's policy, while North American-ness got in the way when differentiation from the United States and American policy was sought. Today the British, having chosen to become a European country, stand in attitude midway between North America and continental Europe, much as, according to Lipset, Canada stands midway between the United States and Britain.

The tone of moral certitude that characterizes public pronouncements by Canadian and American politicians alike is appropriate to the circumstances of the continent's settlement. It was the promise of a holier or a better life, or both, that brought the early settlers across the ocean. The agnostic Tom Paine could speak of America as 'the asylum of mankind.' Paine, like so many others of his time, could summon Nature to support his claim that America was different. 'In no instance,' he wrote, 'hath nature made the satellite larger than the primary planet, and as England and America, with respect to each other, reverse the common order of nature, it is evident that they belong to different systems. England to Europe, America to itself.'[18] Herbert Hoover echoed the theme when he declared that 'through three hundred years Americans had developed something new in a way of life of a people which transcended all others of history.'[19] North America, Prime Minister John Diefenbaker proclaimed, could send forth 'a message for all mankind' – 'the North American experience of harmonious relations.'[20]

The conquistadors bringing salvation to, and taking gold away from, what is now Latin America were very different from the hard-working people who settled temperate-zone North America. The Protestant ethic of English-speaking America was more consonant with industry, trade, and profit than with glory, power, gold, and diplomatic advantage. There may be only a loose connection between the sometimes pharasaical posture of moral superiority and the expediential practices of North American economic diplomacy, but the need to couch foreign policy pronouncements in language that would win public approval gave them a moralistic and often a genuinely moral tone.

However high-minded their public statements about war and peace, the two countries' leaders were before 1939 careful not to promise military support to the prospective European victims of aggression. As late as 1936, Mackenzie King, far from allowing Canada 'to speak decisively,' asked rhetorically: 'Do the honourable members think that it is Canada's role at Geneva to regulate a European War?'[21] In November 1940, on the eve of his election to a third term as president, Franklin Roosevelt promised in the Democratic party's Irish-dominated Boston stronghold that he would never send an American boy to fight in a foreign, i.e. European, war. (Of course, the war was no longer foreign once the United States had entered it.)

The possibility of 'normal' participation in the Europe-centered international politics of that era was excluded as a matter of faith and morals. As before 1914, so it was before 1939. As war approached, some of the pacifists and isolationists suddenly became willing to wage a crusade so that 'never again' would future pacifists and future isolationists have to wage a similar crusade. As it was in 1919, so it was in 1945. The North Americans were the strongest in their belief that a world constitutional convention could repeat the Philadelphia miracle of 1787 (and the analogous Canadian miracle that began at Charlottetown in September 1864) and start the world off on a whole new basis.

Protracted wars are characterized by an inversion of ends and means. At first, victory is sought as a means to achieve the ends originally thought worth going to war for. Then, as victory proves elusive, politicians and publicists begin to ask what war aims will evoke the extra measure of support that will lead to victory. In the North American tradition they are well equipped to respond. To peoples that eschew 'normal' participation in Europe's wars and diplomacy, that may join in crusades but are otherwise basically isolationist, the elaboration of utopian war aims comes easily.

For example, in James A. Macdonald's 1917 book, *The North American Idea*, a one-time clergyman and former managing editor of the Toronto *Globe* explained that the North American idea was 'the Right of a Free People to Govern Themselves' and that the 'free expression of the North American mind' was giving Europe its second chance.[22] We may smile indulgently at such assertions of moral superiority and their use to justify North Americans joining in Europe's wars. The North America of the Two had been at peace for a century, and the expectation of war across the American-Canadian border had been close to zero for half a century. But in their relations with each other had the two countries established a pattern of behavior that policy-makers in other countries would find it feasible to emulate?

Self-congratulatory celebrations of the centennial of peace along the Canadian-American border stopped abruptly in 1914, but the First World War strengthened North American beliefs that the European operators of a system of power politics that had produced that bloody and protracted conflict had few lessons to teach the North Americans who had bailed them out when their system failed. There was renewed interest in discovering the reasons for recurrent war in Europe and peace in America, and in discerning what it was about North American political behavior that could help the world. Believers in 'the North American idea' during the First World War rationalized their support for it in some such terms as O.D. Skelton advanced in 1915: Canada was not in the war, as it had been in the Boer War, as 'a testimonial of affection for the mother country but [as] a realization of our duty and of the cause at stake.'[23] This was consistent with his earlier (1909) statement in support of binding arbitration: 'America has set Europe an example of common sense in international relations.'

Others too, before and after the war, saw compulsory judicial settlement and binding arbitration as providing the way to peace. The president of Columbia University, Nicholas Murray Butler, produced in 1913 *The International Mind: An Argument for the Judicial Settlement of International Disputes* and encouraged the young William Lyon Mackenzie King to form a Canadian Association for International Conciliation parallel to the already existing American association.[24] As prime minister of Canada, King in 1923 was to describe the International Joint Commission as a 'new answer to old world queries as to the most effective methods of adjusting international differences.'[25] He quoted approvingly President Warren G. Harding, who said, 'It is the public will, not force, that makes for enduring peace ... In a new world point of view that is in very striking contrast to the old world attitudes of the past.'[26] The North American idea might have fared better in Europe if the United States had joined the League of Nations, but such was not to be.

The 25-volume series of studies on Canadian-American relations sponsored by the Carnegie Endowment for International Peace is, however, a tribute to the strength of the idea, as Carl Berger has shown in a retrospective essay on that series.[27] This huge binational scholarly effort is indeed a consequential part of the history the series illuminates. Its organizer and general editor, James T. Shotwell, an Ontario-born Columbia University historian and, like Columbia's President Butler, a leading figure in the Carnegie Endowment, had been the general editor of the monumental 150-volume series The Economic and Social History of the World War. If that series was meant to demonstrate the folly, irrationality, and unimaginable cost of the First World War in terms of wealth and human misery, the Canadian-American series, Berger suggests, was meant to demonstrate the wisdom, rationality, moral superiority, and feasibility of the North American way of living together. There was both naïveté and profundity in the animating idea behind the Canadian-American relations project.

The two countries of North America are an odd couple, with so atypical a bilateral relationship that North American homilies before and after the First World War on how well neighboring states can 'adjust their differences' if they will only follow the North American example fell on deaf ears, particularly in Europe. There may, however, be one lesson other pairs of new nations that are immediate neighbors can learn from the Canadian-American experience. For almost a century, when the United States was young, its Department of State was housed in modest quarters and even spent the decade before 1875 in a wing of the Washington Orphan Asylum. What is now the Department of External Affairs in Canada had its beginning over a barber shop on Sparks

Street in Ottawa. When sites had to be chosen for border fortifications in the aftermath of the War of 1812 and the exact location of the New York–Quebec boundary line had therefore to be determined, President James Monroe himself went up from Washington to look into the matter. The friendly authorities on the two sides of the border then decided to set up a joint commission to recommend a final demarcation. The commissioners recommended a line that incorporated the errors of the original surveyors so as not to inconvenience residents of the border area.[28] New states, this experience suggests, should keep their foreign offices small and their foreign policy concerns practical, especially those that relate to their nearest neighbors. They would do well to let private transnational relations flourish and lighten the burdens placed on public diplomacy.

Even among pairs of adjacent states unequal in population and gross national product, a class one group of Canadian scholars has called 'disparate dyads,' Canada and the United States are an odd couple.[29] In most regions of the world other than Europe one outsize state is dominant.[30] In contemporary western Europe, as in the old European state system in the days of Europe's glory, there are several leading powers and about a dozen others. The Soviet Union is big in relation to its eastern European and Middle East neighbors, as is the Chinese People's Republic in eastern Asia, India in southern Asia, Nigeria in western Africa, South Africa in southern Africa, Brazil in South America, and the United States in North America. In all but one of these regions, the international political subsystem consists of more than two states. Only Canada lies alone in a separated part of the world beside a single great neighbor. It is no wonder that its government tries to reduce Canada's vulnerability to and dependence on actions taken by the United States by pursuing trade policies meant to diversify its international commercial relations, by being a signatory to the North Atlantic Treaty and cooperating in NATO, by being the seventh in the seven-sided economic summitry of recent years, and by strenuous participation in public international organizations.

What are remarkable, and distinctively North American, are the conditions that have made the greater coercive power of the United States almost irrelevant in the management of intra–North American affairs. Canada lies alone and in close embrace with its neighbor. Alan Gotlieb, Canadian ambassador to the United States, has described the two countries as living together in a state of 'marital compatibility.'[31] This does not preclude heated exchanges and episodes of infelicity that look like marital incompatibility. As Georg Simmel, in his discussion of the sociology of the two, noted, an enduring and respectful relationship may be built on differentiation of function.

Without pressing the metaphor too far – John Holmes referred more circumspectly to the two countries' 'common law life in North America' – we should remind ourselves that there is a *déjà-vu* look to the 'equality of respect, differentiation of function' aspect of the relationship. The United States is the second of Canada's mates. Canada's leaders had learned from their experience with Britain: 1 / to shy away from formal institutions that pledge Canadians in advance to accept in a crisis decisions with which they might disagree and therefore to avoid schemes for imperial councils of defense; 2 / to shy away from sideshow military enterprises that first-ranking powers with world-wide interests might choose to embark on; and 3 / to move easily in circles of influence in the other country.

The ways in which Americans and Canadians occupy the continent they share are as significant for understanding

North America's position in the world political system as for understanding their relations with each other. Geographers define the ecumene as that part of the living space that is occupied and in contact with the other occupied parts. A map of the world showing all the land areas within ten miles of a highway, railroad, navigable river, canal, or airport in one color and all the rest in another would show dense uninterrupted patches of ecumene in Europe and in North America.[32] In both continents there are ecumenes that spill over man-made international boundaries. The forces of nation-building in earlier centuries and of national self-determination in the era of mass literacy have produced in Europe a maze of sovereignties in which, except for the German-speaking parts, ethnic and political boundaries now largely coincide. The identity problem that is so often said to exist in Canada seems in Europe unreal and remote.

In North America English-speaking Americans who live north of the Mason and Dixon line and west of the Hudson River and Canadians who live west of Quebec sound very similar to each other – more like each other than like their own countrymen in other regions. Further, large groups of Canadians and Americans have more in common with each other than with some of their own fellow nationals – in, for instance, Quebec and the southern United States. Carl Berger reports that one graduate student at the University of Chicago wrote in 1906 to his former professor at Queen's University that he had begun 'to realize the significance of what you often said to us – that the boundary line is imaginary, and that really the people of Ontario and New York state have far more in common than the people of Ontario and Quebec.'[33] All this poses a problem for Canadians who put a high value on preserving and promoting what is distinctive about their country, or at least their part of it. In the largely uninterrupted ecumene of North America, each Canadian part is a separate northern extension of the connected mass lying south of the border, and the biggest, central chunk of Canada's part of the ecumene is ethnically split.

The Canadian-American boundary has, however, stood the test of time. Among the world's international boundaries it is relatively old. Those of continental Europe – Franco-German, German-Polish, Italian-Yugoslav, Czechoslovak-Hungarian, among others – have been redrawn in the twentieth century, most of them more than once. The wars of South America in our time have all been over disputed borders. While the Alaskan-Canadian boundary dispute, settled eighty years ago, was an uncomfortable final reminder of what has happened in Canadian-American relations when push came to shove, the border between the two countries is now set. Even the absurd and inconvenient anomaly of Point Roberts, the tip of a peninsula attached to British Columbia that is American territory only because it is south of the forty-ninth parallel, is unlikely to be corrected. With the boundary that divides North America precisely drawn and fully legitimated in the eyes of both countries, the basic relationship of stable inequality may be said to have jelled.[34]

The nineteenth-century technology of highways, canals, telegraph systems, and especially railroads made big states possible in North America. It was one prerequisite to the creation of a transcontinental Canada, the other being non-annexation by the United States. The new technology permitted people, goods, and messages, including governmental directives, to move quickly and relatively cheaply over long distances and facilitated the creation of two big states, each larger than the whole of Europe west of Russia. To the two huge countries it helped bring rapid economic development.

In Europe the consequences of the new technology were vastly different. Long-established and powerful nation-states in such a densely settled region were not going to be dissolved by the new technology, but its benefits affected them unequally. It strengthened Germany, then being consolidated in the heart of Europe, and later the sprawling Russian Empire and its Soviet successor.

That the canals, railroads, hard-surfaced roads, telegraph systems, and tunnels under the Alps came long after the multi-state great power system was in place meant that their political effect was mainly on the distribution of power among established states in Europe and between Europe and the rest of the world. The new technologies were themselves incapable of creating a United States of Europe (or of western Europe), or any other entity of a size, population, and GNP comparable to those of the United States and Soviet Union. Western Europe was bound, therefore, to become in a matter of decades a region of second-tier powers. The differential effect of the new technologies in terms of power and influence reinforced the advantages that the Soviet Union, the United States, and Canada enjoy through being on the periphery of the conflict zone of the European powers.

Although the European balance-of-power state system assured for centuries, until the eve of the Second World War, the survival of the small-power neighbors of Europe's great powers, it had no comparable success in preventing war and therefore in preventing boundary changes that reflected the fortunes of war. Unlike the 4,000 miles of Canadian-American boundary, particular boundaries in Europe have been repeatedly moved back and forth to record victory and defeat in periodic wars. Europe entered the twentieth century littered with ethnic groups that saw themselves as on the

73

wrong side of a frontier, often because some long-dead ruler had had to pay for a lost war by ceding a province. No such irritants of irredentism survive in North America.

Old boundaries, it is said, are good ones. Interests become adjusted to and built up around them, even if they were arbitrarily, imprudently, or unjustly drawn. It is no longer relevant that when the British were negotiating boundary agreements with the United States, colonial interests were not always vigorously defended (except for the concern not to be involved in a war in which the colonies might be overrun and perhaps annexed). Trouble will not come along the border because of any pressure to relocate the land boundaries.[35]

Among the other pairs of neighboring states of grossly unequal power – the Soviet Union and Finland, Germany and Austria, Germany and Denmark, Britain and Ireland, the United States and Mexico, India and Pakistan – Finland, Austria, Denmark, Pakistan, and Mexico have all been invaded by their great neighbors in the twentieth century. The Irish had to fight a bitter war to bring an independent Irish state into being.

Only the Anglo-Irish pair bears comparison with the American-Canadian, and then only in certain dimensions. Ireland is not well located to receive military assistance in case of trouble with Britain, but being within a zone of international peace its need to call for help to meet a British military threat seems remote. Population and GNP ratios are much like those of United States and Canada: in the ten-to-one range. The movement of people, goods, capital, and ideas between Britain and Ireland is about as free as between the United States and Canada. There is no language barrier, despite efforts to resurrect the Gaelic tongue. Irish television may have trouble attracting viewers away from its British competitors – a situation parallel to Canada's. Yet the differences between Anglo-Irish and American-Canadian relations are profound and will remain so, at least until the troubles cease in Northern Ireland and memories have dimmed of the period when Britain treated Ireland more like India than Canada.

On matters of detail the bilateral relations of Canada and the United States no doubt have examples both positive and negative to offer to other clusters of neighboring developed countries with comparable social systems and political ideals. The United States and Canada in their turn may find it useful to know about successes and failures in the management of relatively open borders where they exist, as among the Nordic countries, among the Benelux countries, between Germany and Austria, and between Australia and New Zealand. It would be useful to make an inventory of small successes and small failures, of problems identified and solutions attempted, to assist in the management of relations between countries that have or wish to have open borders with each other. It would not, however, carry us far in our effort to discover the North American-ness of the North America of the Two.

One feature unique to the Canadian-American relationship complicates it in a fundamental way. The Finns, Irish, Danes, and Mexicans have no identity problem. Canadians, at least English Canadians, do. This reduces the relevance of the North American experience to European and Europeanized parts of the world. The new nations of Africa, the Pacific, the Caribbean, and western Asia may, like Canada, have identity problems; but they are so unlike Canada in almost every other respect that the Canadian-American relationship in the 1980s contains few lessons for them.

It may be useful to compare Canada with Ireland, Finland, and Australia. The Irish have serious problems, but few of them doubt that they are Irish or wonder whether there is such a thing as Ireland. Writers and artists do not worry that success in competing in the London marketplace of ideas and creative art will compromise their Irishness. If Finland had a Swedish-speaking majority and a Finnish-speaking minority, its problems of nation-building and reconciliation of its two ethnic groups would be more like Canada's. One way the Australians demonstrate their sense of identity is by calling the English 'Pommies.' Canadians have no comparable word for demonstrating that they are not Americans; but they too make use of symbols of counteridentification, particularly in foreign policy. 'Independent' for them means not just foreign policies that are freely chosen; it may also mean made-in-Canada policies and even policies deliberately different from those the United States has chosen.

In the late 1960s and the 1970s the Canadian debate about disengagement from responsibilities in Europe for Western security and over economic policies designed to lessen dependence on and vulnerability to events in the United States afforded a wide opportunity for the expression of anti-American sentiments.[36] In the 1980s portrayal of American policy as a cover for the greed of the 'military-industrial complex' or, alternatively, for the multinational corporations and depiction of the United States as a fading empire may be combined with cogent criticism of seemingly wrong-headed American policies and of the clumsy use of American power in support of those policies. One does not have to be anti-American to evince skepticism about somewhat frenetic anti-Soviet rhetoric, high spending on the American armed forces, and political-military adventurism in both near and far places; but there is a form of anti-American Canadian nationalism that predisposes those who exhibit it to discover that 'Uncle Sam has gone and done it again.'

Concern about American wrongheadedness and clumsiness ought to be distinguished from Canadian irritation with American insensitivity to what Canadians are thinking, saying, feeling, and doing. Imbued with a sense of world mission and supreme confidence that such right-thinking fellow North Americans as the Canadians would support them, American decision-makers may neglect to inquire in advance as to Canadian views. Prickliness, wariness, and outbursts of anti-American sentiment are natural Canadian reactions. The intensity of some Canadians' search for national identity in terms of what is either wrong in the United States or distinctively right about Canada is backhanded testimony to pervasive North American-ness.

The habits that make it easy for Canada and the United States to live side by side peacefully and to their mutual benefit cannot be readily exported to other parts of the world. In the Third World boundaries are often new and artificial, nation-building has not yet proceeded very far, and the network of trade and transportation is rudimentary. In the Second World, Soviet troops crossed into neighboring countries in 1956, 1968, and 1980. (Who knows what will happen in 1992?) In the other main part of the First World, formal supranational institutions and protectionism entirely unsuitable for North America have been built within the European Economic Community.

Still, in the most general sense the North American experience can be seen as an example worthy of study elsewhere. The two countries have shown that sovereign neighbors can get out of the habit of making war on each other. Conflicts among neighbors can be resolved or at least alleviated without building elaborate supranational institutions. Boundaries can divide settled areas without enormous loss of productivity and without leaving embittered irredentist minorities on one or both sides of an international border. Canadians and Americans have demonstrated how respect for diversity permits contention over inevitable differences to be carried on within the context of a common North American-ness. They have shown that there can be a balancing process in the politics of an international region even in the presence of a stable imbalance in power if the nations of the region are pluralistic societies, a point to which we shall return in the next chapter.

5 / Limited partnership for peace and security

The argument in this chapter is simple. Americans and Canadians have learned how to handle their purely North American affairs well enough that they are free to collaborate closely in the management of North American 'external affairs.' They will do so, however, only when their two governments both find it advantageous and especially, as in many issues of North American security and world peace, when the Canadian government finds it almost essential. We therefore pursue four themes: the post-isolationist basis for limited partnership; what makes the present stable imbalance in North American politics persist; how meeting the two countries' joint needs with respect to the outside world is reconciled with meeting Canada's special needs as the less powerful partner; and what happens when the need for close collaboration does not seem pressing.

The unbreakable peace between the United States and Canada is a cause rather than a consequence of the way Americans and Canadians settle their problems with each other in the management of their shared continental homeland. Many in both countries learned the wrong lessons from the paeans of self-praise generated before and after the First World War about a peace that only the most maladroit politicians could have broken.[1] The 'right' lessons would have been about how to realize the full benefits from a continent-wide zone of assured peace, some of them economic and some the consequence of shared concerns about relations with Europe and the rest of the world. The wrong lessons were about the shining example of peace North Americans set for the war-prone peoples of Europe.[2] That Europe had only to follow the North American example to become another huge zone of assured peace was a fundamentally isolationist notion.

Many of the issues in North American external affairs about which the two governments now find it prudent to act together relate to North American security, the security of western Europe, nuclear arms, and the deterrence of a third world war. In the days of isolationism there were no security issues perceived in either Washington or Ottawa as matters for coordinated decision-making.

Since 1945 peace and security have posed an unending series of choices for North Americans. The Canadians know that the Americans will fill any decision-making vacuum.[3] Washington has no license to speak for Ottawa, and vice versa; but common sense suggests that the government that commands ten times more human and material resources than the other will play the larger role in planning and providing for the defense of North America. This tells us little, however, about how much or what kind of share Canadians will have in the decision process, how big and what kind of sacrifice Canadians will make in executing decisions about North American security, or how different those decisions will have been as a result of the roles played by Canadians.

The onset of the Reagan administration brought a chill to Canadian-American relations, arising primarily from differences over the management of the North American economy.[4] The 1984 elections in the two countries, by contrast, signalled a warming trend. The climate for collaboration in security matters was, however, unaffected by such weather changes.

The ratio of resources sets a limit to what Canadians can do about American policies regarding North American and western European security, the nuclear arms race, and East-West relations generally. The case is different in the asymmetrical interdependence of the two economies and societies. Canadians can do something about this asymmetry. By their national policies they can to some extent insulate the Canadian economy against the effect of major events in the giant American economy. For more than a century, at least since the inception of Sir John A. Macdonald's National Policy, they have done so, even at some cost to the Canadian standard of living. Canadians will continue to have to make hard choices between policies designed to exploit fully the opportunities of a continental economy and those meant to maintain mastery over the Canadian part of that economy.[5] The Canadian government's choice to keep its borders so open as to permit a high degree of informal economic integration is as much a part of the relationship as the relatively small role American coercive power plays in continental political and economic processes.[6] Canadian choices on the openness of the common border have a significant indirect impact on measures to promote North American security; but the two streams of decision-making are quite separate.

Stable imbalance and the persisting small role played by coercive power are two ways of describing the same pattern of behavior. The imbalance is stable because the American power card is kept face down in American-Canadian relations about North American problems. If it were turned up, there would be no North American security problem. Canadians would have a security problem, but their number one threat would be from the United States. The Americans would have a security problem, but the United States would not be defending Canada when it defended itself. Understanding what keeps the stable imbalance in internal North American affairs stable is fundamental to understanding how North American external affairs are managed.

What, in addition to the legitimacy added by time, makes it persist? There is no constitutional alternative that the two governments calculating separately would each decide was superior to the present organization of the continent into two sovereign states of unequal magnitude. Talk about American annexation of Canada petered out early in the twentieth century, and involuntary annexation is today not even an imaginable alternative.[7]

What about a voluntary merger of the two federally organized sovereignties into a North American super-federation, and what about a more modest alternative, the organization of a North American community along the lines of the European Economic Community? Voluntary merger may be ruled out almost as quickly as involuntary annexation. Nobody is proposing it, a federation of the two federations would not work, and a proposal to create a colossal federation of fifty states and ten provinces seems even more far-fetched than a federation of federations.[8]

What about a European Community type of solution? It would seemingly do less violence than federation to interests that are distinctive to each people, but such a scheme may also be ruled out quickly. The EEC's Big Three – France, West Germany, and the United Kingdom – can be counted on to check each other in a way that makes it safer for a smaller power to join than if there were only one big member. There would be no such check on the United States in any North American supranational organization with real power. Canada could not hope to exercise the degree of influence or sense of identity it now has as a sovereign equal in a two-state subsystem. Clearly then, North America will not go the way of the EEC. The two sides of the North Atlantic have remarkably little to teach each other about managing continent-wide interests, even though the people of the two continents have similar basic values, social systems, and levels of technological advancement. And this is the case for both purely continental problems and problems with the outside world.

The absence of a feasible alternative is a negative explanation for the present pattern of Canadian-American relations. More positively, the interests of the two countries are in major respects perceived as enough alike or so compatible that they do not strain a power imbalance that otherwise would be irksome to Canadians and tempting to Americans. Both countries benefit from treating the security of North America as an indivisible whole. Both benefit also from the complementarity of their economies, which makes a high degree of informal economic integration appropriate. Common interests and a consequent predisposition to agree and to collaborate cannot, however, be the whole explanation.

We have used the terms *power*, *coercive power*, and *military power* loosely and at times interchangeably. Not all coercive power takes the form of control over the machinery of violence. Not all power is coercive; people can be persuaded or offered economic inducement. Power is not like money in the bank, equally useful for any purpose for which money is useful at all; some forms of it may be useless for gaining one objective and indispensable for another. In the broad sense of the word, power is as important in the political processes of

83

the North America of the Two as in the World of the Big Two; but its currency and distribution within the North American subsystem are in some ways like its currency and distribution in the domestic politics of stable wealthy democracies everywhere. In most ways they are unlike those prevailing in Soviet-Western relations. The role of power in any set of interstate relationships can be defined in three dimensions: conflict vs consensus; public (government to government) vs private (person to person); and vital interests vs interests deemed less than vital.

In areas in which national (or subnational) interests are perceived on each side as shared or compatible, superior power will not be invoked because there is nothing to invoke it for. Where transborder relations are expected to remain private and unregulated or are regulated by entities other than the two national governments, the stronger state's superior capacity to punish and to grant or withhold favors is irrelevant. Since great powers do not fritter away the coercive power that makes them great on issues that their leaders do not regard as vital, the vital–non-vital dimension may limit the role of coercive power, producing restraint on the part of the more powerful even if the bilateral relationship is not particularly amicable, and great restraint if, as in the Canadian-American case, it is.

Along all three dimensions, the room for the American government explicitly to invoke its superior capacity to coerce is small. Transborder relations are largely private. Where they are not private they may be regulated by understandings among neighboring local, state, or provincial authorities on the two sides of the border. Many problems of North American governance are regulated by ad hoc arrangements between opposite numbers in the two federal governments who deal directly with each other rather than through standard diplomatic channels. Even where a problem is handled through regular diplomatic channels – with the Canadians particularly careful to be precise if only because the United States is so big – overlapping value systems offer each country many opportunities to state its position in terms of what may seem fair to both sides and few occasions to state them in terms of what that country is in a position to insist upon. Issues on which agreement does not prove possible, such as earlier Canadian measures to control Arctic pollution, are rarely if ever in the category of vital interests – the defense of North America, issues of peace and Western security, and the forestalling of a thermonuclear Armageddon.

Not surprisingly, Canadians often show greater awareness than Americans of the inequality in power that lies below the surface of apparent bargaining equality. Lurking suspicions of improper and unacknowledged exercise of American power are all the greater because of the real difficulty in distinguishing between the coercive effects of deliberately exercised power and the effect in Canada of private decisions taken in the American economy.

Canadian nationalists who exhort their countrymen to be brave and support a policy that Uncle Sam might not like – a few may even urge them to support a policy *because* Uncle Sam will not like it – are generally right in one respect. Uncle Sam will do little more than grumble, however wise or foolish the particular policy and however irritating to the US authorities, if indeed they notice the irritant at all. There was grumbling combined with pointed advice when Canada announced its National Energy Program, which, though apparently not meant to be anti-American, was so interpreted in Washington.[9] When first announced in October 1980, it seems to have been as much of a surprise to Canada's representatives in Washington as it was to the Americans.

Anti-American Canadian nationalists will not accept the description in the preceding pages of a relationship characterized by the sparing use of coercive power by the United States. They are not impressed by the absence of military coercion by the American government. Neither would the Norwegian sociologist Johan Galtung or other advocates of 'positive peace,' who are also critics of so-called informal imperialism. The 4,000-mile frontier is in the view of such critics a frontier of 'structural violence.' An 'invisible continent of non-territorial actors,' including intergovernmental organizations (IGOs), international nongovernmental organizations (INGOs), and business international nongovernmental organizations (BINGOs), jeopardizes 'positive peace.'[10]

Under the militant banner of 'peace research' those who speak of structural violence are telling Canadians and the world that there is not real peace in North America because private international transactions across the frontier of structural violence take precious things away from Canada without truly compensatory return. This perspective contrasts sharply with that of those who believe that the outstanding characteristics of the frontier are its openness and the impossibility of war breaking out between the two states on either side of it. It is from this latter perspective that we look briefly at how North American political processes, both governmental and nongovernmental, work with respect to matters internal to North America. The informal as well as the formal processes provide the context in which North American political processes regarding the world outside operate.

A balancing process does go on in the continent's politics even if the two states are stably unbalanced. In the pluralism of North American politics groups on one side of the border

86

are constantly finding allies on the other; the whole northeast of the United States is, for example, as much afflicted by the acid rain problem as is eastern Canada. Their common problem is primarily the soft coal burned in the Ohio valley power plants. Canadians are a minority of North Americans, but they are by no means the only vigorously self-conscious minority engaged in consciousness-raising activities to affirm the value of the group and to improve its prospects for survival and future satisfactions. The other minorities – racial, ethnic, regional, economic, sectoral, religious, subnational, transnational, and so forth – do not form a separate state; but all of them depend upon a differentiating sense of self-worth and an integrating respect for diversity, characteristics they share with a group of 25 million North Americans who call themselves Canadians.

These other minority groups, 'non-state actors,' cannot themselves conduct foreign affairs, a monopoly of governments; but some have views about the world outside North America and significantly influence the behavior of foreign policy-makers. Many stake out positions for which they seek government support. In so doing, even when they do not directly affect either government's behavior in foreign policy they affect the two governments' capacity to identify and work harmoniously on those external issues on which there is a North American interest to be promoted. The often untidy clash of interests among private, local, and sectoral non-state actors tends to take a form that keeps them off both governments' 'high politics' foreign policy agenda. Open societies divided by a rather open common border are bound to reveal clashes of interest and communities of interest that do not follow international boundaries and to confound efforts to settle the clashes by reference to differing perceptions of the two countries' national interests.

Structural violence and informal imperialism, though normatively ambiguous phrases with pejorative overtones, refer to important facts in North American economic life.[11] There are indeed a host of 'non-territorial actors' in political-economic competition, but 'informal integration' is a less loaded term. Not all these nonterritorial actors are BINGOs. Among the nongovernmental decision-making structures are trade unions, and a great majority of Canadian union members belong to 'international,' i.e. American-Canadian unions, in which they are a minority.[12] The Canadian tail can, however, sometimes wag the American dog, as happened in Chrysler's wage negotiations in 1982–3.

The fence along the boundary is not very high, and, so far as the two economies are concerned, there are many gates in it. Some, though not all, private economic interests support the existing consensus on both sides that the fence should be kept low. The politics of adjusting conflicts among these economic interests goes on both within the two countries and across the common border. Thus, the attitudes and interests of big-city North America and the agricultural interior of the continent may be more at odds with each other than the attitudes and interests of Canadians as a whole and Americans as a whole.

A local or sectoral interest group may be quick to invoke the assistance of its own national government if the opposing interest is on the other side of the border. Such a group is almost certain to claim that a national interest is served by protecting its particular group interest. Maine potato growers and Canadian radio and television producers are in this respect not different.

The clash of subnational interests lying on opposite sides of the border is not very different from the clash that occurs when opposing interests are on the same side of the border, except for the greater ease with which the special interests can in the transnational clash wrap themselves in the mantle of asserted national interests. There are 535 members of the two houses of the Congress of the United States, most of whom have more than half a million constituents to be pleased or displeased by the way his or her representative supports his or her perceived interests. Individual senators and representatives may raise a hue and cry about Canadian acts of omission or commission that seem to serve that representative's constituents poorly. Canada's representatives in Washington then face difficult choices as to how deeply to become enmeshed in the domestic American political process.

Special interest group pressures to build up, or sometimes to tear down, the dividing wall between the two countries are not contrary to the national interest just because they are sectoral or local. Not all of them are the pressures of Canadians frantically trying to stop the seepage of things American through the wall, though protectionist demands no doubt come more naturally to producers in the smaller and less developed country. Pressures have arisen from 'anti-Continentalists' and others with a genuine concern for the viability of Canadian institutions judged important to maintaining and promoting the richness, variety, and distinctiveness of Canadian life, including Canadians' sense of Canadian-ness.[13]

Americans should have no quarrel (though some do) with Canadian public policies that in the interest of civic education and cultural nationalism regulate the percentage of Canadian content of the mass media or otherwise favor Canadian interests in their competition with American interests.[14] Neither should they object to the conditions the Canadian government sets for participation in the joint defense of North America that maintain the integrity and separateness of Canadian units operating under their own commanders. If there is as a result some loss in the efficiency of the North American economy or defense arrangements, so be it. Efficiency cannot be an end in itself, even in the conduct of North America's external affairs, given the pluralism of the two societies and the existence of two nation-states.

Meanwhile, Canadians and Americans benefit from the efficiency that comes from leaving in private hands so large a share of decisions as to who does what with an effect on the other side of the border. They penetrate each other's countries very freely by world standards, and the penetration is two-way.[15] Although Americans have invested far more in Canada than Canadians have in the United States, the per capita investment of Canadians in American enterprises is greater than the per capita investment of Americans in Canadian enterprises.

Opinions differ widely as to the equity and efficiency of the untidy North American political-economic processes, but Canadian-American economic relations are not generally perceived as, and in fact are not, so unambiguously exploitative as to impair the ability of the two countries to collaborate in the pursuit of peace and security. The high degree of informal integration of the two economies and the clash of private interests in cross-border politics that is somewhat like the clash in domestic politics in each country ease the problem of keeping the conduct of the continent's external relations separate and manageable. They also help keep the two governments' relationship stable under the difficult conditions of imbalance.

To maintain this happy state of affairs has required disciplined forbearance on both sides. The Canadian government has ordinarily taken care not to be a bad neighbor, and the

American government has not often yielded to the temptation to link unrelated issues in the hard bargaining that is inevitable when close neighbors have many problems to be sorted out and points of friction to be smoothed over.

Wary Canadians know that Canada must not be a bad neighbor. Power and size are not unimportant, and the United States has historically been freer to be a bad neighbor.[16] It still is, though more often through inadvertence, inattention, or insensitivity than because Canadians' and Americans' priorities are not in accord. In the 1970s and 1980s much of the American 'bad neighbor' behavior has been in the area of the environment, which has encouraged an anti-American alliance of those concerned about threats to the environment with those concerned about nuclear power, the nuclear arms race, cruise missile testing in Canada, and new nuclear weapons in Europe.[17]

Not to be a bad neighbor is a policy that antedates Confederation. For both good British and good Canadian reasons, the British took care that their North American colonies not provide the occasion for a third Anglo-American war. Canada has less need in the 1980s than Britain did in the nineteenth century not to appear to be a bad neighbor, but the prudent Canadian practice has been to pluck only a modest number of the American eagle's feathers at any one time.[18]

The imbalance in Canadian-American relations, though stable, is not idyllic. Canadian prickliness and American insensitivity are likely to remain for a long time, but perhaps there is a mechanism that permits this insensitivity and prickliness to be manifested whenever safety and solvency are not threatened but somehow suppresses it when the going gets rough. It works something like a thermostat. One illustration of its operation is to be found in the series of events that began with Ford Canada's plan to sell to the People's Republic of China items that Ford in the United States could not have sold to China. The Canadian government took exception to what appeared to be American efforts to make the writ of the United States run in Canada too.[19] The Diefenbaker-Eisenhower agreement of 1958 was negotiated when the two sides had each decided that a continuance of the dispute was unprofitable. So long as this mechanism operates, the two countries can work together for whatever goals regarding the outside world their governments share.

Not being a bad neighbor is the characteristic Canadian contribution to making an unequal relationship tolerable. On the American side, forbearance takes the form of 'nonlinkage,' i.e. of not using superior power to grant or withhold what Canadians value in one area as a means for gaining their compliance or acquiescence in another. It is another name for the practice of leaving the power card face down. Linkage is fraught with danger for either country. If practiced by Canadians, it would encourage the United States to respond in kind, and Canada would not win.[20] If practiced by the United States, historical precedent suggests that it would intensify the Canadians' search for counterweights to what they would see as arbitrary uses of American power.

Nonlinkage comes naturally: value systems in the two countries overlap, and superior coercive power is irrelevant when agreed values point the way toward settlements regarded as fair by both parties. This situation reinforces the habit of not trying to make package deals that trade concessions in one area for concessions in another. It is further reinforced by the pluralism of both societies. In negotiations between states that recognize that a primary national interest is to protect a myriad of regional, sectoral, and private interests, none of these interests can readily be sacrificed as a way of promoting another.

The American government cannot sell out West Coast fishermen to get a better deal for East Coast fishermen. It could not have abandoned its support for Americans who feared serious injury by Canada's Foreign Investment Review Agency in exchange for a guaranteed supply of Alberta's superior light crude oil to refineries in the Middle West that have been idled by Canada's restrictive policies on oil exports. Similarly, Canada cannot back away from supporting a position on international rivers important to British Columbia so as to get the Americans to expand trade opportunities for producers in Quebec or the Maritimes. One does not find a parallel to the effort of Senator Jackson and Representative Vanik to link American agreement to the expansion of Soviet-American trade with Soviet agreement to ease restrictions on the emigration of Jews.

Hints of linkage have not, however, been entirely absent. In the 1950s Secretary of State John Foster Dulles mentioned in the same conversation a possible reduction of American oil imports from Canada and his opposition to Canadian efforts to universalize membership in the United Nations by means of a 'package deal' that Dulles opposed.[21] In September 1981, Myer Rashish, then undersecretary of state for economic affairs, spoke ten days after President Reagan and Prime Minister Trudeau had discussed, without agreeing about, certain aspects of Canada's National Energy Program. He warned that Canadian energy and investment policies might lead to American retaliation and spoke of 'risks of irreparable damage to the bilateral relationship.'[22] There seems to be no case, however, in which unresolved problems in security were linked to threatened sanctions in any other area, or vice versa.

Finally, we should note again the infinite variety and multiplicity of relations across the border. Under such circumstances, coherence by either country in its policies toward the other is an unattainable goal.[23] Issues have to be settled one by one, if at all, and on their merits rather than by presumptive assertions of power. The contrast with Soviet-American relations is sharp; lack of common values tends to mean that bargains are struck not on their merits but, if at all, by an exchange of concessions, as in the Helsinki Accords.

Mutual forbearance helps to explain the workability and durability of the pattern of collaboration in North American security affairs. How do we explain the super-power–middle power partnership in security affairs from the opposite direction? What makes the North American subsystem in world politics work well enough to satisfy influential groups in and out of government in the two countries? We may begin by asking about the satisfactions it affords Canadians. The most obvious is the one with which we began: the de facto 'security union' makes both countries safer. This is a necessary but not a sufficient condition for the present division of labor in making and executing decisions to endure; other ways of sharing responsibility might also provide adequately for the security of North America. We must therefore ask how well the present arrangements meet the special needs of Canada.

Canada is not helpless. It is a consequential player on the world stage and an essential partner in the solution of many North American security problems. Moreover, Americans have a huge economic stake in Canada that is hostage to satisfactory Canadian-American relations. At the same time most Canadians are realistic and see their country as the smaller and necessarily the more adapting partner in matters in which the two governments have to act together.

In an earlier era, when isolation and low defense budgets were still possible for both countries, Canadians had far fewer occasions to observe manifestations of American military power and to be sensitive to the political implications of having a country ten times bigger next door. If Canada were more nearly equal to the United States in population and GNP, Canadians' concerns about their country's status and its ability to control its own destiny would disappear, and the North America of the Two would operate on different principles. If Canada were a genuinely small power, with a population and GNP very much smaller than one-tenth of that of the United States, Canadian leaders would know their place. Canada might be a species of North American Denmark, and there would be fewer occasions to consider problems of status and autonomy in the country's diplomatic calculations. Perhaps the prevailing ratio of size and power between the countries maximizes Canadian sensitivity to such problems.

Canadian sensitivity may be heightened by a special form of American insensitivity. John Holmes has reminded us of Adlai Stevenson's sage comment, that the instrument Uncle Sam needs most is a hearing aid. Daniel J. Boorstin and Alan Henrikson have pointed to Uncle's hyperopia, his bad habit of overlooking his near neighbors.[24] Canadians have trouble getting Uncle Sam either to hear them or to see them, and he has a tendency to act as if he spoke for Canadians too. To the extent that that is true, he makes them into disfranchised North Americans.

Canadian sensitivity, often intensified by American insensitivity, complicates the process of finding common or compatible policies on North America's external affairs. The resulting costs and benefits for each country's objectives in foreign policy remain to be assessed in detail.

We shall next consider how the two governments meet any jointly recognized need for policies to achieve a common objective in a whole range of North American relations with the rest of the world. In North America, unlike western Europe, the burden of proof is on the proponent of integration. Autonomy has a higher priority for Canada than it has for any single country in the European Economic Community. It does not preclude cooperation, but the demand for it greatly influences the form that needed cooperation will take.

In whatever common enterprises the Canadian government finds it essential to act along with the United States, concerns of status will not be permitted to stand in the way. Where there is genuine choice – and in many areas this is unconstrained by the difference in scale of human and material resources – and even where close collaboration is unavoidable but choice is substantial as to respective contributions, something like genuine equality in bargaining capacity is the rule. If either party holds back, there is no deal. Each side determines how much of a price it is willing to pay and how much value it puts on maintaining or promoting the common interest at stake. One would not expect the bigger partner to be prickly about its status and autonomy or to be acutely sensitive to the status and autonomy concerns of the smaller. The complex and protracted negotiating over the construction of the St Lawrence Seaway illustrates the point.[25]

Canadian diplomats are said, particularly by Canadian participant-observers, to be more pragmatic than their American counterparts. American pronouncements in foreign policy are likely to reflect what Hans Morgenthau in *Politics among Nations* called 'nationalistic universalism' and others have called 'global isolationism.' John Holmes could report that with respect to the United Nations and other international organizations created during and after the Second World War the Canadians 'had strong reasons for satisfaction in seeing the Americans entwined in world organization – not sufficiently, however, to let the Americans get away with assumptions about their unique mission as God's temporal power on earth.'[26] With their modest human and industrial resources pragmatic Canadians have reason to pick and choose carefully and reassess continuously both their reach and their grasp.[27] Otherwise, Canada might be towed along and tossed about in the wake of the mammoth American ship of state. Charles Ritchie was expressing not only a professional diplomat's perspective but also a pragmatic Canadian view when he wrote, 'I see policy as a balance, also a calculated risk, as the tortuous approach to an ill-defined objective. All-out decisions, unqualified statements, irreconcilable antagonisms are foreign to my nature and to my training.'[28]

On issues about which Canada is in the end almost bound to follow the American lead – effectively or ineffectively, whole-heartedly or half-heartedly, unreservedly or warily – its negotiators press the Canadian view when it differs from the American, but they press it pragmatically, not to the breaking point.[29] On many of those issues, such as those connected with air and missile defense, Canadians can be confident that in the end the Americans will do whatever they deem necessary to ensure that the combined North American effort is sufficient to meet a threat to the continent. Canadians must accept the overall American decision, but they are still able to make an independent judgment as to their own contributions. They may choose to buy into the American decision process by undertaking to share in the human and material costs of particular decisions. They may choose to share in the cost so as to preserve their self-respect. They may choose to add on to the American effort in ways that make the program as close to Canadian preferences as possible. To change the metaphor, the Canadians may be able to fine-tune big American decisions about the defense of North America, but they do not have the option of changing the song.

These observations apply almost as much to the defense of western Europe as to the defense of North America itself. Over the years and through many changes in leadership the two countries have continued to agree that both their countries will be more secure if western Europe is made more secure. Here, as with North American defense, Canada has the possibility if not of a free ride at least of reduced fare. It does not have to, and it does not, allocate as large a share of its GNP for North American and western European defense as the United States does; but it does allocate enough to have a voice in the development, deployment, and employment of forces to defend North America in North America, the North Atlantic, and Europe. The Americans can cajole, explain, scold, and harass; but the decision as to the level, form, and direction of the Canadian contribution is as much Canadian as the decisions about the American contribution are American. Thus, in fulfillment of its NATO commitment, Canada has chosen to play an especially large role in anti-submarine warfare in the North Atlantic. As with the Canadian homeland itself, Canadians can be confident that whatever the Americans choose to do for their own security by way of defending western Europe, they will also be doing for Canadian security.

Prudence, not fear that American power may be turned against them, dictates that Canadians recognize the ultimate responsibility of the Americans to make and to implement certain major decisions relating to the defense of North America. Even here, however, the Canadians do not forgo the right to be kept informed, to be consulted, to propose, to express misgivings, and above all to set the level of their contribution and the conditions of its use.

In areas of foreign policy other than security for North America and western Europe, Canadians have no reason to be afraid of being hard bargainers or of going their own way. The serious questions about where and when they should stand up to the United States relate not to the risk of doing so but to the occasions on which it would have been, is, or may be in the Canadian interest to do so. The costs of adopting a tough bargaining stance may be greater for the Americans because Canadian sensitivities to being 'leaned on' are greater and because Canadians tend to pay closer attention to the consequences for Canada of what the United States is doing than vice versa. As Prime Minister Trudeau pointed out in his public letter of 10 May 1983, which appeared in leading newspapers throughout Canada, responding to some 7,000 expressions of concern about cruise missile testing in Canada, the United States is the only super-power many Canadians can figure out how to hold responsible.[31] That fact increases the cost to the United States of pressing the Canadian government beyond the point that it can readily carry public opinion along with it.

Status sensitivity and Canada's concern for maintaining control over its own destiny have long affected relations between North America and the rest of the world. Being 'unpaid Hessians,' said Lester Pearson, was not a tolerable status for Canadians whether it was the British or the Americans who called the tune.[32] He echoed Mackenzie King's complaint in the Second World War that 'these people ... from the Old Country ... seem to think that all they have to do is to tell us what is to be done.'[33] The other dominions, as they moved toward self-government, did not have Canada's special problem, that posed by a huge neighbor threatening cultural absorption. The Canadians' need for seeing themselves and for being seen to be making made-at-home policies has been great and has reinforced what would in any case have been a skillful and determined protection of Canadian interests. Given Canada's heritage of status sensitivity vis-à-vis Britain, avoiding the appearance of being taken for granted by the United States was bound to be a Canadian concern. In the 1962 Cuban missile crisis, which involved decisions to put the North American Air Defense Command on an advanced state of alert, many Canadian authorities felt that they were not apprised of the developing danger and of the proposed American response in time to express the Canadian view in a matter threatening both North American countries.[34]

Exhibiting status sensitivities and engaging in other consciousness-raising activities have not, however, accorded with another long-standing Canadian practice, maintaining a low profile with a small peacetime defense expenditure and periodically making reference to Canada's limited capabilities. There is Laurier's classic statement at a colonial conference that 'we have no complaints and very few suggestions.' There were minuscule appropriations for the armed forces in the 1920s. There was Prime Minister Bennett's hand-wringing assertion when he asked in 1933: 'What can someone representing only ten and a half million people do?'[35] More recently, there was Canada's quiescent role in 1979 when NATO embarked on the dual-track strategy of seeking arms control advances while planning to place new intermediate range missiles in Europe.

Maintaining a low profile does not always mean being inactive in diplomacy. Thus, at San Francisco, when the language of the United Nations Charter was being negotiated, hotel corridor diplomacy served Canadian interests better than the grandstanding, headline-grabbing diplomacy of Herbert Evatt served Australian interests.[36] It has been hard for Canadians to convince themselves that most of the rest of the world sees their country as more independent than they do themselves; that the United Nations Reconstruction and Rehabilitation Administration put Canada on the map for those who had not already noticed it; that its very status as a middle power, with a corresponding lack of taint of the super-power and a wide reputation for humaneness, made it in much of the world's eyes the trusted and trustworthy northern country; and that its miraculously good first generation of professional diplomats optimized its influence.

Hardly anyone questions the twin principles that in two-state North America there must be equality of respect and formal status and at the same time a 'weight of counsel ... dependent on function rather than power.'[37] Thus, it is not inequality in the overall power relationship per se that makes it appropriate for the United States to have the steering oar in North American security matters but the ability of the United States to perform the larger share of the security function.

The Americans, however, have been very slow to respond to Canadian status sensitivities. Item: at Paris in 1919 they persisted in interpreting Canada's demand for a full role in the new League of Nations as giving something called 'the British Empire' two votes, and perhaps even six, since, it was said, one would have to do for the other dominions and for India whatever one did for Canada. The possibility that Canada might be a second North American vote – ironically it turned out to be the first – never entered the Americans' heads. Item: Canada, as we noted in the third chapter, received no invitation to participate in the Washington Conference of 1921–2, though the conference was a triumph for

101

Canada, and in the American interest, too, since it brought an end to the Anglo-Japanese alliance. Item: Washington excluded Canada from certain war councils in the Second World War, explaining that otherwise Brazil and who knows who else would have to be included; this despite Canada's major role in the war. Item: Harry Hopkins proposed that in the food councils set up during the war there should be either a British or a Canadian representative, but only one 'British Empire' vote.[38] Item: Dean Acheson proposed a territorial division of responsibility in the Far East between the United States and 'the British Empire,' as if Britain's and Canada's interests could be lumped together. The Americans were astonishingly slow learners with respect to that old bugaboo, the hydra-headed empire that could stuff the ballot-box in international organizations.

The Americans were equally slow to recognize the separateness of the inter-American and North American subsystems in world politics; the two in fact have little in common except that the United States is part of both. For good and sufficient reasons Canadians have usually shied away from entanglement in the Washington-centered Organization of American States, just as they did from the London-centered imperial federation schemes, and just as they will from any other grouping in which Canada could become committed in advance to enforcement action that at the moment of crisis it might not find in its own interest to support.

The British were slow learners too. In January 1944 Lord Halifax, in a speech in Toronto, spoke of establishing 'the united empire to match the strength of the United States'; he still envisioned a London-centered imperial defense system in which Canadian human and material resources would be pooled with those of the rest of the empire.[39] Canadian objection to article 10 of the League Covenant should have

102

warned against any awkward reincarnation of such schemes.[40] Canada's concern at San Francisco about article 44 of the UN Charter demonstrated how enduring is its resistance to imprecisely defined commitments. There is something North American about this, as is shown by the circumlocution embodied in article 11 of the North Atlantic Treaty and in various other post-war treaties of alliance to which the United States is a signatory. Article 11 provides: 'This Treaty shall be ratified and its provisions carried out by the Parties in accordance with their respective constitutional processes.' Interested American Congressmen were thus promised that in the hour of crisis Congress would still have the power to decide. Americans should be able to understand when Canadian prime ministers fend off pressures to commit Canada in advance by intoning: 'Parliament will decide, when the time comes.'

Since in North America no formal supranational arrangement is possible in which Canada would yield its absolute right of veto, parallel action and informal access to each other's decision-making processes are the standard routes by which the two countries develop or fail to develop common policies toward the world outside.[41] The main prerequisite for effective parallel action is a highly developed 'civic order,' in which the collective activities of businesses, churches, and other active participants in society are independent of detailed direction from either government.[42] Such a transnational civic order tends to generate parallel perceptions of problems and to foster solutions to problems that can be implemented only by common action. Thus, in GATT, the broad consensus among Canadians and Americans enables the two groups to discover the basis for trading concessions with each other.

Even where there is common recognition of some inescapable task of North American defense there appears to be a

103

strong preference for parallel action coordinated by full consultation. General Charles Foulkes, chief of the Canadian General Staff, is said to have placed a high value on his 'Brad' and 'Rad' relations with General Omar Bradley and Admiral Arthur Radford, during their respective periods as chairman of the American Joint Chiefs of Staff. Similar value systems, the need to plan for the security of a shared continent, access to much the same body of information, and close interaction among higher-level military personnel have meant that parallel action usually works.[43] It works for two reasons: because policy-makers in the two countries recognize that North America has lost its insularity; and because the North American need to cope with the threat of world war and the Canadian need, as the less powerful partner, to share in decisions with decisive consequences for Canada's future have been largely reconciled.

Canadian and American decision-makers are not always wholly agreed as to how much of what kind of armed force should at any given time be kept ready and as to where, when, and how it should be deployed or ordered into action. They do not make identical assessments of external danger and of who should contribute what to meet a danger both groups acknowledge is real. Thus, Canadian policy-makers who see some particular American policy as rash and therefore dangerous to the friends of the United States as well as to its foes will not make Canadian forces available to implement that policy. Neither can they be expected to establish identical priorities in foreign policy or always to agree on the most efficient division of labor when both accept the need for collaborative action.

Nevertheless, the United States and Canada have had little choice but to cooperate as they adjusted to a new kind of world, in which a major concern was a war in which a Soviet enemy might deliver a devastating blow directly on North America or indirectly threaten it by action against or intimidation of western Europe. The North American military potential previously thought unnecessary and even undesirable in peacetime now has to be drawn on to maintain ready forces at all times. Since the tasks are great, the resources available for defense not unlimited, and lead-times long, incentives are strong to make efficient use of the resources the two countries choose to make available to the common defense. Thus there is more strain toward efficient collaboration in the defense of North America and and the West than in any other matters involving the world outside North America.

Collaboration on common defense can go forward while the two countries follow quite separate policies on other matters. The pressure for closely coordinated policies is much less, even when the two governments are pursuing much the same objectives. Where there are substantial differences, or where there is no threat to attaining a common objective if the two governments pursue separate paths, Canadian decision-makers have little reason to lock on to American formulae and Americans little reason to press for identical Canadian policies.

North America is one of the world's breadbaskets, and the wheat that either country sells to, for example, East Germany or China reduces by that much the wheat that the other could sell. Competition in grain sales, however, need not interfere with joint defense arrangements and may indeed help to dispel any image of Canada as a cat's paw for imperial America.

In most areas not related to North American security, and in some that are, official relations between the United States and Canada are carried on, as we have said, on the basis of complete bargaining equality. But what happens when easy access and close consultation do not work, and a one-on-one confrontation with Uncle Sam seems inappropriate to Canadians? Here, 'the functional principle' may operate. It is a guide to Canadian policy-making that relates Canada's strengths to Canada's decisions about setting priorities in undertaking international responsibilities, about seeking to share in international decision-making, and about promoting Canadian national interests. Its mysteries and implementation are not always well understood by outside observers, but it provides a rationale for both action and inaction, for both abstention and vigorous participation, and for both acquiescence and persistent maintenance of a distinctive Canadian position.

Canada is not compelled to follow the United States into every corner of the earth in which Americans become involved. The super-power may not always be able to pick and choose, but the somewhat less universally responsible middle power can.[44] It has a considerable range of choice in deciding where to focus its attention and on which issues to exercise its substantial but not unlimited influence and about which to seek access to high-level decision-makers in the United States. As Pierre Trudeau said to an American audience in 1982: 'We, your friends and allies, recognize that some decisions only the United States can make; equally, however, there are decisions that require consultation and a sharing of responsibilities. As friends, we have a duty to hold up the looking glass in which you see yourselves.'[45]

Canadian decision-makers expect Canada to stand with the United States in a supreme crisis and find it prudent to make this clear. But they also expect to be informed and consulted even about decisions in which they recognize that the Americans have the last word. Prudence also would seem to dictate to the Canadians that strongly expressed American preferences should not be lightly ignored. However, the lesser power's picking and choosing can include many areas in which Canada does not wait for the United States. Lester Pearson, for example, was the first foreign minister of a NATO power to go to Moscow. In opening up relations with the People's Republic of China, Canada was one step ahead of the United States; in wheat sales, in gaining permission for journalists to visit, and in diplomatic recognition Canada acted first.

Prime Minister Trudeau's 1978 proposals to the United Nations for 'suffocating the arms race,' however sensible and creative, fell on barren ground and were not for a while pursued in the absence of any American expression of interest. They were, however, made a matter of record before Canada accepted the two-track proposal for the introduction of intermediate nuclear weapons into western Europe. This may exemplify Ambassador Charles Ritchie's observation that the Canadian ambassador to the United States must learn how to 'put things in a way which does not offend and yet disturbs.'[46] Prime Minister Pearson's 1965 Temple University speech, in which he gingerly advocated 'a pause' in the American bombing in Vietnam 'at the right time,' disturbed the easily offended President Johnson, but it demonstrated the opportunity a Canadian leader may have to give a lead when American opinion is split.[47] Pearson was holding up the looking glass about which his successor was later to speak.

The most frequently cited illustrations of the functional principle relate to Canada's active and often leading role in conference diplomacy and international organizations. Certain aspects of this multilateral activity are relevant to a discussion of the external affairs of the North America of the

Two. What begins as a North American question may, for example, be moved toward resolution by converting it into a world question of setting new standards of behavior for states everywhere. Mobilizing countervailing influence outside the bilateral relationship has on occasion proved useful when the United States has not been ready to agree to Canadian proposals. One example is the Canadian effort to deal with Arctic pollution. The United States had strongly protested Canada's Arctic Pollution Control policy, which was meant to prevent a repetition of the experimental transit of the Arctic by the oil tanker *Manhattan*. The matter was vigorously pursued by Canada in the law-of-the-sea negotiations.[48]

Avoiding one-on-one confrontations with the United States by negotiating in a multilateral setting is a standard principle of action in Canadian diplomacy. Thus, the Canadians have felt more comfortable in helping defend western Europe within the framework of NATO than they would have merely on the basis of a bilateral agreement with the United States. However, as John Holmes wryly observed, active participation in NATO did little to help Canada with 'bilateral continental issues,' for 'the old world was not much interested in being called upon to reduce, for Canada's sake, the imbalance of the new.'[49] The not very effective Contractual Agreement with the European Community (1975) and the frequent references to the third option, a policy of reducing dependence on the United States by diversifying trade relations as expounded by Mitchell Sharp (1972), of which more was heard in the early Trudeau years than subsequently, further illustrate the pursuit of 'outside options' in Canadian diplomacy. Third options help reduce the sense of uneasiness Canadians may feel about not fully reciprocated dependence on the United States. They also serve both countries' larger foreign policy purposes. The more the outside world is enabled to see that Canada can and does act independently the more useful it can be as an alternative supplier of diplomatic initiatives. Lacking the taint of the super-power and therefore thought capable of disinterested actions, it is enough like the United States to be useful as a conduit or even a proxy when there is a chance for an opening in East-West relations.[50] During the Vietnam War Canadians facilitated some communication between Hanoi and Washington, beginning in 1965. Outside North America Canada is perceived as sufficiently similar to the United States to be able to provide North American–type goods and services. Also it can reflect enlightened North American ideals of the obligations of wealth and international distributive justice and take initiatives that might be closed to the United States.[51] One example was Prime Minister Trudeau's co-chairmanship of and Canada's active role in the Cancun conference of October 1981 on North-South relations.[52] In taking advantage of opportunities of this nature, the Canadian government does not become a surrogate for the always suspect super-power but rather the means by which an authentic element of North American opinion finds expression in the world at large.

In the relatively few formal bilateral organizations that the United States and Canada have created to deal jointly with common problems, decision-making powers have been held to the minimum. The International Joint Commission, which for many decades dealt almost exclusively with matters related to boundary and transboundary waters, has an equal number of Canadian and American members; its two national sections are organized separately; and its output is primarily in the form of fact-finding and recommendations.[53] The Permanent Joint Board on Defense (PJBD) is also a two-section commission with power to recommend rather than to act and with a record of keeping its agenda modest.[54] Implicit recognition that the larger country had wider interests in the promotion of which formal consultation with Canada would be unfunctional is to be found in some of the PJBD's practices.[55]

We have described the United States and Canada as involuntary conscripts in the struggle to ensure that the balance of nuclear terror in the world will not be overturned and that the balance of power will be stabilized. Yet even in this almost unavoidable collaboration the North Americans have employed few formal bilateral agencies, and their members have usually carried out their functions in a very informal fashion.[56]

NORAD (originally the North American Air Defense Command, now renamed the North American Aerospace Defense Command) is the one binational formal organization on which Canada and the United States have conferred authority to give orders. Its authority is not to make policy but to execute it and is meticulously circumscribed. In the absence of the American commander-in-chief his Canadian deputy has all the authority lodged with the commanding officer. This arrangement reflects the inescapable fact that Canadian skies must be monitored if either country is to have any air and missile defense at all. The agreement has been renewed from time to time, usually at five-year intervals.

Mutual forbearance, easy access, frequent consultation, non-linkage, Canadian wariness and cultivation of third options, and quasi-domestic treatment of subnational and transnational interests form the context for parallel action to provide for the common defense of North America and to promote certain other common interests. Crude power analysis might suggest that the Americans would always have their way. Because Canada and the United States are not political monoliths, however, there is a tug and pull of sub- and trans-national interest groups and a high capacity for trans-national consensus and informal integration. In the conduct of North America's official external affairs the two governments' capacity for parallel action and their distaste for formal integration are paradoxically but understandably high.

The burden of making the unequal but stable relationship work falls most heavily on the Canadians, and they have borne that burden with notable success. They have not, however, completely escaped from either of two recurring dilemmas: one posed by the simultaneous hunger for status and determination to keep commitments to a minimum; and the other posed by the wish to avoid one-to-one confrontations, which has involved the cultivation of third options, while maintaining special access to and maximum influence on American decision-makers.

The two dilemmas are not unrelated. Multinational organizations provide Canada a means to satisfy status hunger, while it takes care to be a low-profile good neighbor, to keep prior commitments to a minimum, to maintain a low defense budget, and to preserve easy access to the highest levels of American decision-making. Even in NATO, however, Canada runs the danger that the North Atlantic security system will assume a dumbbell shape with the United States at one end and all but Canada at the other.[57]

6 / Prudence, morality, and the range of North American choice

In the conduct of foreign relations, American and Canadian leaders, like politicians everywhere, reconcile as best they can what they believe is desirable and what they think is possible. Misperceptions may lead to unwise, sometimes monumentally misguided, estimates of what is possible. North Americans were both slow to perceive their continent's loss of insularity and slow to accept the logical consequences of that loss.

George M. Wrong's was a lone voice when in 1909 he wrote Laurier: 'Canada occupies a position of world importance and has in her hand the power to shape world history' and went on to advise the prime minister that 'if Canada speaks decisively, Germany will in time see that with our future what it is the race is hopeless.'[1] Sir Wilfrid evidently thought that his country might have to wait a little longer for its influence to be decisive when he declared: 'The twenty-first century belongs to Canada.'

Premature assertions of world importance aside – and there have been many in both Canada and the United States – no leader in either country could get far out in front of public opinion, and any chance there might have been of deterring either world war by North American preparedness and guarantees was missed. The general notion that Canadians and

Americans can and ought to deter a possible third world war gives contemporary leaders a wider range of choice than their predecessors had before 1939 as to how, where, when, and to what extent their respective countries are to engage in deterrent activity.

Decolonization and disimperialism have wrought as great changes in North-South relations as bipolarity and nuclear weaponry have in relations among the powers of the first rank. These changes also pose a wide range of questions for the leaders of the two stable, wealthy North American democracies as they ponder the counsels of prudence and the calls of conscience in their dealings with the Third World, but the width of their range of choice depends on the degree of public understanding of the changes. Matters were very different before 1939 and even more so before 1914.

British diplomats, according to John Hay, American ambassador to Great Britain during the Spanish-American War and subsequently secretary of state, vowed 'their slavery to Canada.'[2] In Washington their working days were largely spent on problems of Canadian-American economic relations.[3] Elihu Root, Theodore Roosevelt's secretary of state 1905–9, took the initiative in 'cleaning the slate' of outstanding problems in Canadian-American relations; and James Bryce, Britain's brilliantly successful ambassador to Washington 1907–13, cooperated enthusiastically, paying visits to Ottawa at least once a year. In the management of affairs internal to North America the 'low politics' of trade and investment have continued to bulk large in relation to the 'high politics' of war, peace, and the pursuit of power. This is in accord with a Whiggish tradition in British diplomacy, but it is also a natural North American state of affairs, given the

113

interdepence and intimacy of relations between prosperous and culturally similar neighbors dwelling in a zone of firmly established peace.

Historically, the emphasis on economic diplomacy has gone hand in hand in the United States with anti-colonialism and 'informal imperialism.' Somewhat paradoxically, anti-colonialism in an ideologically pure form and a system of informal imperialism – based on the Monroe Doctrine, the 'open door,' a capability for intervention by American Marines, and precepts of international law related to the 'denial of justice' – have flourished alongside each other. Why, Americans might have asked, pay for an expensive colonial system when one can apparently have all of its economic and most of its political advantages at a very low cost? In the case of Canada the cost to Americans was nil. The door was already open; American lives, liberty, and property were as safe in Canada as at home. Canada was almost as open to the American trader, investor, and manufacturer as was the American west. Less-developed Canada, like the less-developed American west, was 'informally imperialized' to a degree that by any rational calculation made annexation, particularly of the involuntary sort, seem counterproductive. Meanwhile Canadians were asking why they should pay for elaborate imperial defense schemes that would not protect them from the United States when the United States would protect them from everybody else. On both sides, low politics set the agenda for relations with the other side. It still does for intra – North American international relations. The case is different and often more difficult with respect to relations with the rest of the world.[4]

Most high-politics theorizing about international relations is meant to clarify choices in diplomacy and strategy among first-ranking powers in their relations with each other. It is not often directed toward explaining distinctive behavior within the North American subsystem. Canada and the United States are no different from other states in generally putting survival interests ahead of principled interests. Canadians are not concerned, as everyone knows, that in some future war Canada and the United States might be on different sides. They and Americans do not differ, except perhaps in the greater intensity of the American concern, about the need to cope effectively with a perceived Soviet threat and over the need to deter a third world war. Canadians, however, tend to see the survival of their country and its distinctive characteristics as less threatened by wars and threats of wars than by internal disunity, North American cultural homogenization, or both. Concerning the first fear there is testimony in a prime minister's diary. 'Our own domestic situation,' wrote William Lyon Mackenzie King in 1935 after a cabinet discussion of sanctions against Italy because of its invasion of Ethiopia, 'must be considered first, and what will serve to keep Canada united.'[5] The comment is dated, but the concern is not. However carefully Canada's powerful neighbor maintains an official relationship of sovereign equality and ceremonial respect, the second fear will also not quickly disappear.

Canadians' perception of a threat to their country's cohesiveness bears no comparison with that which faced Americans when Abraham Lincoln was running for president, but it reflects far more of a concern than exists in the United States of the 1980s with respect to its dissatisfied minorities. The black and Hispanic minorities are each about as numerous as the whole population of Canada. Perhaps Americans ought to be concerned about their country's cohesiveness, but the large American minorities are not territorially concentrated, and neither of them is a 'founding people.' Unlike

115

the French Canadians of Quebec, they are in no position to organize separate political institutions.

A federation as loosely articulated as Canada's is probably harder to break than one that confined the country's vast and varied provinces in a tight federal grip. Let us consider how loose federation and Canadian concerns about national cohesiveness and 'informal annexation' affect the choices that the leaders of either or both countries make regarding the rest of the world.

As prime ministers, Sir Wilfrid Laurier and Mackenzie King pursued policies that kept within strict bounds London's capacity to count in a crisis on any particular kind or amount of support from Ottawa. The conscription issue was finessed by having in effect one mobilization policy for Quebec and another for the rest of Canada. Good will was strained between the parts of Canada that benefited from the protectionist National Policy, such as Quebec with its clothing and shoe manufacturing, and the parts of Canada that produced largely for export but had to spend the dollars so earned on high-priced protected goods of Canadian manufacture. Such features of Canadian policy before 1939 have their counterparts in the post-1945 period, even though Canadians, like Americans, have long since abandoned the notion that nothing needs to be done about the world outside until the moment of crisis. How much these domestic preoccupations still limit the resources that Canadians are willing to invest in foreign policy cannot be measured, nor can the extent to which they skew the pattern of such foreign policy 'investment' as does take place; but the effect cannot be trivial.

Canadians may also differ from people in some other countries in the vigor of their efforts to advance Canada's middle-power status concerns 'on the cheap.' In spite of a relatively low mobilization of the country's great economic potential in support of Canadian foreign policy objectives, their leaders have had some success. It is not only that Canadians and Americans have tended to let danger rear its head first and then prepare to meet that danger or, in Lord Hankey's words, that Canada could be counted on to help in a genuine crisis only 'if the Canadians thought it was a real crisis, if they could send help in time, and if that help would make a difference.' But note also the relatively low percentage of Canada's GNP allocated to the armed forces, the assistance given as tied aid so that Canada's generosity is largely recycled back into Canada, and the reduction of Canada's military contribution to NATO in the late 1960s.

Austere analyses of the comparative stability of a two-power and a five-power world à la Kenneth Waltz cannot by themselves provide useful guidelines for North American policy-makers.[6] There is no such thing as an average super-power, an average great power, an average small power, or, for that matter, an average state. Hypothesizing about model worlds and codifying the behavior of states class by class, with emphasis on the behavior of first-ranking powers, are essential exercises in theory construction. But the general habit of not regarding a class of one as a class and the general aversion to thinking of states of unequal power in a particular subsystem as a class have left gaps in international relations theory and thus limited its direct relevance to understanding North America's role and behavior in the world.[7] And these ways of thinking do not clarify the choices available to Washington and Ottawa.

The point must not be overstated. Classical realist and geopolitical theory, buttressed by contemporary neorealist and strategic theorizing, does indeed help define the limits of choice open to North American leaders in an age of air and missile power in which one state in Mackinder's World Island is too big for the others on that World Island to balance. The passing of the European age in world politics has not meant the coming of a North American age. That apparent possibility was an illusion created by the circumstances of 1945 in which the United States and Canada, alone among advanced industrial countries, emerged from the war with their productive industrial and agricultural bases intact. What most sharply differentiates the new age, of the 'peripheral powers,' i.e. two super-powers both outside western Europe, from the preceding is the recognition in North America that whatever needs to be done about the threat of a third world war needs to be done in advance.

Events of the twenty years after 1919 demonstrated that the new order created by the Treaty of Versailles could not be maintained without North American support. Perhaps what is more important, they demonstrated that that new order could not be maintained peacefully without a prior North American commitment firm enough and credible enough to deter even a Hitler.[8] Such a commitment was forthcoming from neither the United States nor Canada before 1939. Only since 1945 have the two governments been willing to engage in coalition planning of the kind that might have staved off the Second World War. They have backed up their firm and detailed promises about the maintenance of Western security by keeping North American forces in Europe for four decades. The signing of the North Atlantic Treaty in 1949, formalizing the new relationship between North America and western Europe, was final evidence that the insular era in North America had passed. The day of the League of Nations–type advocate of collective security against any aggressor anywhere as a way of coping with great power aggressors, whichever state it might turn out to be, had by 1949 passed as completely as had the day of the isolationist. The new belief in Canada and the United States was in collective defense against an identified aggressor. Prudential calculation, not a sense of world mission, keeps North America's guarantees of European security intact and its armed forces deployed to give credibility to the guarantee.

In this age of the peripheral powers Canadian and American perceptions of their respective countries' roles in the world were bound, however, to suffer some deflation after 1945, as the countries ravaged by the fighting rebuilt their economies. Prime Minister Trudeau, when he assumed power in 1968, declared that Canada had a problem of adjustment with respect to its foreign commitments, one of 'getting back to our normal size.'[9] It took the trauma of the Vietnam War for Americans to begin debating what to do to 'get the United States back to normal size.'

The process was aided and accelerated by the growing understanding by Americans that their near-monopoly in intercontinental air and missile nuclear weaponry had been replaced by a Soviet-American duopoly. Coincident with the new arrangement was an era of 'indiscipline' in both the Western and the Soviet camps. The French in Europe and the Chinese People's Republic in Asia broke ranks. Big limited wars in northeast and southeast Asia turned out to be impossible to win and difficult to stop. Third World states meanwhile were growing less and less coercible. The oil-producing countries of the Middle East demonstrated both the economic and the political vulnerability of North America and the West to oil embargoes and price manipulations. Leaders of less developed countries were learning how to appear on the world stage as claimants for income transfer rather than as suppliants for economic aid. The North American age in world politics was over before it began. However, the Trudeau government discovered in the course of the 1970s that 'getting back to normal size' is not a formula that identifies large opportunities for disengagement. In the aftermath of the Vietnam War a chastened American leadership made a similar discovery.[10]

Unable to disengage and involved in meeting a commonly perceived threat to security and peace, the two countries are in a symbiotic relationship. In part they are mutually supportive in a way that all members of the Western security system are, including the European members of NATO, plus Japan, Australia, and New Zealand. The North American symbiotic relationship goes further: Canada is not just another NATO ally. Canada's participation along with the United States in the establishment of NATO and development of coalition military plans and deployments to make western Europe secure made the Western alliance system look much more like a genuine North American–western European collaboration than like a Warsaw Treaty–type arrangement between a super-power and its obedient satellites.

The generally symbiotic character of the asymmetrical and unequal Canadian-American relationship is particularly important as it relates to problems of continental defense. The irascible First World War Australian prime minister, 'Billy' Hughes, spoke scornfully of Canadians 'nestling in safety' while they rejected schemes for imperial defense that were attractive to Australians and unattractive to Canadians.[11] Hughes, however, was referring to a fact of North American life. Canada is a privileged sanctuary if only because it is valuable to the United States as a defensive glacis, especially in an age in which only polar regions traversible by missiles and planes stand between it and the Soviet

Union. For one super-power to attack the other by way of Europe is to go the long way around.

By itself, Canada is almost as poorly situated for defending itself by itself against a real Soviet threat as it would be against a hypothetical American threat. The land-resources-people ratio so favorable for Canada's future prosperity is unfavorable to the future security of a Canada standing alone. It needs the support of the United States even as the United States needs to have Canada kept safe. The Canadians have the advantage of not having to be as continually vigilant about the defense of North America as about a great range of other Canadian interests. However, they cannot escape the political problem of how much 'club dues' to pay and to what security club to belong. For their own self-respect and for a ticket of admission to the bodies that make decisions that could greatly affect Canada's future they make a substantial contribution to the common defense.

The privileges and opportunities that accompany sanctuary status are multiple. During both world wars Canada with an unresolved and burning issue regarding conscription could nevertheless safely send huge volunteer armed forces abroad. It could take the lead in North American policy and has sometimes taken it when the American government was hobbled by indecision, congressional resistance to executive leadership, and isolationist opinion. Sometimes Canada has been able to take positions that have made it a kind of loyal opposition inside the North American political system, a better reflection of a substantial element of informed élite opinion in the United States than positions taken by high American government officials. Sometimes – for example, with respect to the Far East in the Dulles period of diplomatic brinkmanship – it has acted to restrain the rigidity and impetuosity of some important American policy-makers.

Lester Pearson's Temple University speech in 1965 on the desirability of halting the bombing of North Vietnam is a notable example of a Canadian effort to tug at the coattails of a headstrong chief executive next door, Lyndon Johnson. In the 1980s, the inflamed anti-Soviet rhetoric of the Reagan administration ideologues, including the president himself, brought a third period since 1945 in which the moderating influence of official Canadian policy-makers combined with that of unofficial critics of that policy on both sides of the border and congressional critics and showed that there is a process shaping the two countries' policies that subjects them to an extra measure of testing and, not infrequently, an extra opportunity for correction.

The question is no longer, as it was before 1939, one of peripheral North America providing centrally located western Europe the additional support it needs to frustrate an aspirant for world hegemony. The core area in the Western military system has moved across the Atlantic to North America. But why, one may ask, include Canada in the core? Isn't the core really only the United States?

One needs to distinguish between 'us' in North America and the more inclusive 'us' of the Atlantic community, comprising not only North Americans but also western Europeans in implementing the North Atlantic Treaty commitment. The promises made by North Americans to western Europeans in that treaty have been implemented by an American nuclear umbrella held over Europe, by American and Canadian collaboration to keep secure the North American core area (the central bastion of Atlantic Community strength), and by the American and Canadian military presence in Europe, without which the North American promises would have lacked credibility. That presence in Europe reflects a serious calculation of self-interest on the part of Americans and Canadians. This prudential calculation and its implementation make it possible to describe North America as the core and western Europe as the periphery in the organization of Western security.

There is another way in which Canada and the United States are to be distinguished from all the rest of those in the Western alliance system. In the calculations regarding the threat of a third world war, Canada's position in relation to the United States is significantly different from that of the other members of NATO. Canada is uniquely consequential in the solving of the problem of over-the-pole super-power competition. The nuclear threat from the Soviet Union, if there is one, is a threat to North America, not one to the United States and Canada separately. The two countries together must be viewed as the core in any nuclear defense or deterrence arrangement.

It is an irony, but also a fact, that North America in the 1980s is more threatened by direct attack than it was at any time between 1939 and 1945. North Americans are left with no choice but to concert a North American response to the over-the-pole threat. Given the propinquity, location, and informal integration of the two countries, does coping with the over-the-pole threat from the Soviet Union exhaust the agenda of almost inescapable Canadian-American collaboration?

This was the sort of question that underlay Canada's great debate in the early Trudeau years about Canada's contribution to NATO and about whether the Pearson–St Laurent Canadian foreign policies were to be maintained.[12] Even during the years of questioning about the magnitude of Canada's role in maintaining international peace and security, Americans and Canadians were probably in wholehearted agreement as to the need to keep as much of the

123

military competition with the Soviet Union as possible on the eastern side of the Atlantic.

As in many other ways, Canadian positions vis-à-vis American policies to maintain peace and security have their parallel in Canadian positions vis-à-vis Britain in an earlier era. The relationship is solid when the chips are down but fragile when it comes to political-military exercises in side-show wars and demonstrations of force in far places. Although there has been a vast change over the last half-century in both American and Canadian attitudes as to what has to be done in advance respecting any major central threat, the Americans have generally thought that their allies, including Canada, should do more than they have done and that the United States has had to do more than it should have had to do. The American attitude is natural for a government with leaders who believe that their country is the one that has to make up for what everybody else has not done. They have had a hard time understanding why Europeans should not contribute more heavily to Western defense. From Prime Minister Trudeau's 1982 reference to 'a growing divergence of views between Europe and *North America* [my italics] and a belief that economic and military burdens are unequally shared' one might have inferred that Canadian defense spending as a percentage of GNP was higher than European and that the Europeans but not the North Americans had been allowing their defense preparations to run down during the 1970s.[13] Both inferences would have been wrong.[14]

Canada's lack of a 'decoupling' problem such as bedevils western Europe and most particularly West Germany makes its relationship different from that of the other NATO partners. European shortfalls in conventional arms open up the possibility that the United States at a moment of crisis would flinch at first use of nuclear weapons in the event that a

Soviet conventional attack could be stopped by no other means. Since there can be no Soviet attack with conventional arms on North America that could not be quickly repelled, the 'first use' dilemma cannot arise with respect to the United States and the defense of Canada.

Canada's security is less closely related to its own level of defense expenditure than is that of the countries in NATO Europe, especially West Germany. Paradoxically, Canada, though the closest ally of the United States, may be the most free of the major NATO members to choose a level of defense expenditures that takes account of the country's other policy objectives. The House of Commons Standing Committee on External Affairs and National Defence heard much testimony on this matter in its 1969 assessment of Canada's NATO policy. The level of defense expenditure Canadians have chosen was in the early 1980s about 2 per cent of the GNP, one-third of the comparable figure for the United States, and its armed forces were 4 per cent of the size of the American. However, Canada has been generous in opening its territory for training exercises and weapons testing by its NATO allies.

To make these observations on comparative budgets for defense is not to say that Canada should spend more or that the United States should spend less. Prudential calculations and moral considerations in the pluralistic North American societies lead to widely varying prescriptions for North American security and international peace. In both countries there are many competing claimants for the tax dollar, and final judgments about sacrifice in the name of national security reflect decisions about how funds not used on defense are to be spent.[15] They could, for example, be put into promotion of some other foreign policy objectives or some domestic policy objective, or they could be left in the taxpayers' pockets. Whatever the political process by which the respective shares and total levels of effort to ensure North American security, Canada and the United States have a shared stake in European security.

In this study the argument has been that western Europe has become a kind of 'North American Belgium.' Just as it was a precept of traditional British foreign policy that the Low Countries should never be in unfriendly hands, so one could say that one fixed principle of 'North American,' i.e. American and Canadian, policy is that western Europe not be under the domination of an unfriendly power.[16] In the pursuit of this objective the salient issue among the North Atlantic allies is the degree of reliance that should be placed on conventional weaponry to ensure western European security. The critical question of defense policy in the mid-1980s would seem to be to create the conditions under which the West and especially the United States would never have to face the first-use dilemma.[17]

Pierre Trudeau offered one good answer to Leonid Brezhnev's challenge to the West to match a Soviet pledge of no first use. He pointed out that both the Soviet Union and the West are already pledged not to use any weapons first by virtue of provisions in the UN Charter.[18] Thus in operational terms the only situation in which the West would be making an additional pledge would be one in which the Soviet Union had already used conventional weapons but had not yet escalated the conflict to the nuclear level. If indeed Brezhnev's real purpose in challenging the United States to match the Soviet pledge was to get a pledge that the United States would not use nuclear weapons if the Soviet Union had first used conventional weapons, Trudeau's response had great political utility. He went on to assert that 'we, the West, ... must rely on nuclear forces' because 'we' have not yet determined to pay the price of repelling the Soviet Union by conventional means. The prime minister may have been hinting but did not quite say that an earlier lack of prudential conventional rearmament narrowed the current range of policy choices. Inability to pay the very high price of making it safe for the American government to follow the Soviet lead in making a no-first-use pledge is different from unwillingness to pay it.

We turn now from a discussion of the dictates of prudence with respect to North American and western European security to discuss more broadly the range of choices open to the two pluralistic, wealthy, fortunately located North American democracies and some of the moral principles applicable to those choices.

Nineteenth- and early-twentieth-century North America had experienced a long period like that of Elizabethan England (and perhaps like that of contemporary Japan) in which the capital base and therefore the military potential could be expanded rapidly because defense costs could safely be kept low. The economics of national security for any country involves calculations of the point at which an additional dollar spent on defense fails to purchase as large an amount of public good as that same dollar would purchase for some other public purpose or would purchase if it stayed in private pockets.[19] Stated in these terms, states do not seek to maximize their power position; states as such do not seek anything, but leaders seek the best mix of the elements in their total value package, including the best mix of preparedness now and power potential husbanded for the future.[20] Treasure and manpower are allocated to overcoming urgently felt constraints, and there was no great fear of attack from overseas in either country during the insular era.

In that era Calvin Coolidge could ask: 'Who are we going to fight?' and Harry Truman could declare that $14 billion was all the United States could afford for defense. Dwight Eisenhower said, when chairman of the Joint Chiefs of Staff, 'There is no security for a country that goes bust.' To Mackenzie King the survival of Canada seemed threatened more by disaffected Québécois than by European dictators. It had been true that there would always be time and always be the United States. However the calculation was made, the peacetime answers in both Canada and the United States were that the level of sacrifice at which another dollar spent for security did not purchase a dollar's worth of public good was low. For both countries, the proportion available for other public or private purposes was correspondingly high, or at least high in relation to that available to the advanced industrial countries of Europe. This proportion was described in an earlier chapter as 'the peace dividend.' Any effort to identify and assess the normative principles that Canada and the United States have applied in their conduct of affairs with the rest of the world must be very largely in terms of how the two governments have chosen to allocate that dividend.

North America has been a fortunate continent for its European immigrants and their descendants, but not always for its aboriginal residents or for non-white and sometimes non-Christian or non–northern European immigrants and would-be immigrants. For much of North American history Tom Paine's 'asylum for mankind' was a refuge only for Europeans and more for some Europeans than for others.[21] One can note the shameful episode of slavery which persisted in the United States long after it had disappeared from other civilized countries, the treatment of native peoples as second-class human beings in both the United States and Canada, selective immigration policies in both countries which reflected prevailing racist theories, failure to act humanely before and during the Second World War as the fate of the

Jews in Germany and eastern Europe hung in the balance, the heartless treatment of North Americans of Japanese extraction in both countries following Pearl Harbor, and complaisance in the 1945 return of refugees from the Soviet Union and Soviet-occupied eastern Europe. All these make a sorry record for two countries of which the leaders in this century have aspired to moral leadership in world affairs.[22] Their record in the second half of the twentieth century is better, particularly with respect to the Vietnamese immigrants of the 1970s. Respect for diversity, a first principle in Canada with its two founding peoples, has taken on new meaning as new Americans and new Canadians have made both countries into cultural mosaics and as 'equal rights' have been transformed from pious preaching into practical politics.

To refer to the historic plight of non-whites in North America is to raise the fundamental question of whether the continent is fortunate because of historic entitlement – i.e. because its inhabitants have what others cannot aspire to have – or because they are exemplars of a goodness in which all the world can ultimately share. It raises the fundamental question of the moral responsibility of the elect who have inherited an especially choice piece of global real estate, of those who declare that they will share their good fortune while the less fortunate catch up, and of the weary do-gooders who suffer from tax fatigue, especially after they discover that foreign aid rarely pays off in gratitude or cooperative behavior.

All may agree that a certain amount of selfishness is morally permissible. North Americans do not, for example, have to stop looking after their own poor until after they have raised the Third World poor to a standard of living equal to that of their own. If, however, they wish to stand on morally

129

firm ground, they must advance no claims and acknowledge no liabilities except on the basis of universally applicable norms.[23] James Eayrs tells us that the first duty of the missionary is to stay out of the cannibal's pot.[24] But how much prudential behavior is justified by that requirement? Americans and Canadians have always saved a generous slice of the peace dividend for domestic consumption and reinvestment. Canada for a century has been building railroads, pipelines, transoceanic cables, and other infrastructures. Canadians have sometimes asserted that these are contributions to the empire's or North America's or the West's security; Canada, they say, must be strong if it is to do its part. Social welfare expenditures and transfer payments to the farmers, to the elderly, and to industries in need of being bailed out have been very large in both countries. Since resources even in wealthy North America are not unlimited, the claims of domestic social justice and self-regarding private interest groups must ultimately be weighed in the same balance with the seeming imperatives of prudence and morality in foreign affairs. Domestic social demands have weighed somewhat more heavily in the Canadian balance.

In democracies foreign policy never has an absolute primacy. The contemporary challenge to priorities that in recent decades have been acknowledged for foreign policy is not peculiar to Canada and the United States and not restricted to political-military matters.[25] It exists everywhere in the advanced industrial world and brings into question policies in trade, aid, and human rights, as well as national security. So-called big-ticket items, i.e. expensive new nuclear or antinuclear weapons systems to be acquired or not acquired, have so dominated a generally uninformative public debate in the United States over defense policy and defense budgets that they have diverted attention from the fundamentally competitive relation between rising social demands and costly non-nuclear alternatives to American nuclear defense of western Europe. They have also diverted attention from claims advanced in the name of international distributive justice and simple human compassion for the poorest of the world's poor. Meanwhile, since astronomical defense budgets make demands at the margins so great that marginal defense items no longer stand in line ahead of every domestic claim on the budget, undramatic but expensive conventional defense requirements tend to get an inappropriately low priority.

At least three economy waves, the first and second in the Truman and Eisenhower years and a third in the 1970s reflecting disenchantment with foreign military adventures after the Vietnam War, have washed over the Pentagon, and others seem bound to follow. The indiscriminate ordering of every big-ticket weapon system in sight in the Reagan years, combined with American budget deficits in the $200 billion range and an 'ecology, anti–nuclear generating power, nuclear freeze' coalition, may reap a whirlwind of reaction. Formidable challenges to the primacy of defense budget items are to be expected periodically.

Canadian decision-makers have exercised quite fully their option of depending on the United States to make good overall deficiencies in the combined North American defense. At least in the Reagan years, deficiencies, if any, relate not to the size of the defense budget but to its composition. Many in the United States and Canada who find it inadequate also find it more than big enough. Defense budgets, however, are not the only measure of how adequately the imperatives of prudence and morality for promoting and protecting American and Canadian interests abroad are being met.

Though prudential (or self-regarding) and moral (or other-regarding) considerations may on occasion point in different directions, they need not always do so. Provisions for regional security arrangements in the UN Charter, for example, show how prudential interest in North American security and moral concern for peace and order in the world at large may be reconciled. The effect of article 51 is to legitimate North American participation in coalition military planning and deployments to defend the North Atlantic and the rimland areas of Europe as well as the western Pacific and the rimland areas of Asia. However, it leaves the United States free, by virtue of its veto power in the Security Council, to prevent the Soviet Union or any other Old World major powers from 'intruding' into North American and New World regional security arrangements.

Some North Americans have derived an inflated sense of goodness from Canadian and American prudential participation in NATO arrangements for western Europe's security, and others have denounced this participation as unnecessary (or perhaps no longer necessary) and as a reckless subordination of the national interest of Canada or that of the United States or of both. In doing so, they fail to meet the argument that the two North American governments have contributed to the defense of western Europe for what its leaders see as good North American reasons. The argument is threefold: it helps to keep the security problem 'over there'; it more than doubles the human and material resources base for protecting interests Americans and Canadians share with Europeans; and it helps to make secure peoples whom many North Americans feel are part of 'us' in a way people in most other parts of the world are not.

To many foreign observers, including Canadians, and indeed to some disinterested Americans, nationalistic universalism or 'global isolationism' – the American urge to fix everything up everywhere in the world, which Franz Schurmann infelicitously called American imperialism – is a marked characteristic of American foreign policy.[26] This may to some extent be a super-power, rather than a specifically American, characteristic; in the official *History of Soviet Foreign Policy* the Soviet Union is described as 'one of the greatest world powers, without whose participation not a single international problem can be solved.'[27] Stated the other way around, the Soviet Union, like the United States, may have lost the capability to ignore or neglect a significant problem anywhere in the world. Whatever the explanation for the American tendency to try to resolve every conflict everywhere in accordance with American premises, the contrast with Canadian behavior is sharp. Selectivity and complementarity are as much the hallmarks of Canadian foreign policy as hubristic universality is of American. Again, we do not need to ask whether this arises from something inherently or traditionally Canadian or is a nearly inescapable middle-power characteristic; it undoubtedly arises to some extent from each.

Selectivity works mostly to provide a rationale for Canada not to do something. With respect to parts of the world other than North America and western Europe, Canadian and American views of their respective countries' responsibilities and interests differ widely. Canada is as averse to joining the United States in limited wars and shows of force in Asia and Africa as it earlier was to joining Britain in similar situations. A corollary is that Canada is less inclined to allocate prudential unilateral military aid geared to the changing fortunes of East-West and Middle East political and military competition and more inclined to allocate funds to support multilateral organizations in providing non-military aid.[28]

The Korean War may be seen as the exception that proves the rule about Canadian selectivity. A UN coat of varnish on an essentially American military operation proved to be just that. The Commonwealth division sent to Korea may have been the last activity based on the illusion that Britain and the old dominions marching along together could be the third in a Big Three World. In any event, the interminability of large-scale limited wars in the nuclear age was not yet well understood when the Canadians reluctantly chose to participate in the Korean hostilities. Thereafter, Canadians seemed determined to leave such exercises for the United States to undertake. Slightly caricatured, the Canadian position might be stated as follows: 'We are not a super-power. As a power of general interest and responsibility you Americans have all the residual tasks; but we don't abdicate our special responsibility to abstain critically when appropriate.' That the Americans may need such criticism from a source that is neither an adversary nor a sycophant is abundantly clear from the record.

Complementarity provides the rationale for doing rather than not doing something. Anti-submarine patrolling in the North Atlantic, 'winterized' contingents for possible use under NATO auspices in northern Norway, a bilingual signal corps to facilitate combined operations, provision of cold-weather missile testing sites, provision of training sites for the armed forces of allies, and integration of Canadian and American territories for the strictly defined purpose of monitoring North American skies against air and missile attack are some of the ways in which Canada has made or can make a complementary contribution toward an objective that it shares with the United States and its other NATO allies.[29]

Complementarity may be just one more name for what experts in Canadian diplomacy call the functional principle. Various opportunities for Canada to do in the world outside North America what it can do best flow from the fact that Canada is not a super-power and not perceived as responsible for leadership in East-West confrontations.[30] Its early prominence in UN peacekeeping activities, Lester Pearson's key mediating role in the Suez crisis, Canada's superior access to the governments of Third World members of the Commonwealth and to the new sovereignties of francophone Africa, and its opportunity (not yet effectively grasped) to promote the interest it shares with the United States in halting the deterioration of liberal global trading arrangements are all cases in which concentrated Canadian effort has been or may be effective.

How is one to explain Canada's benign and largely but not completely unselfish policies in areas other than those involving Canadian and North American security? A mixture of motives seems to account for the active role Canada plays in a variety of international institutions in which the interests being promoted are North American only to the extent that they reflect the humane values that most Canadians and Americans share. Canada's mixed-motive activism seems to be based on a wish, by demonstrating good citizenship in the world, to improve its self-image as it affirms its vocation as a nation and searches for the prestige that comes from being well-regarded; a quest for reduced dependence on the United States by being associated with larger or different groupings than the two-state North American group; a desire to optimize Canada's contribution to achieving objectives it shares with other countries, especially those it shares with the United States, by complementing rather than merely supplementing the contributions of others; a determination to take advantage of the resources released by Canada's semi-protected position to do things good in themselves; and a motivation to play a leadership role in a variety of areas in which the role could be played at a highly affordable price, as, for example, in the lengthy and frustrating law-of-the-sea negotiations and over a long period in UN activities.

The pattern of dignified complementarity enables Canada to get maximum mileage out of its foreign policy dollar provided the situation is such that Canada can 'vote last,' i.e. announce what it is willing to do after those who are making larger contributions have announced what they plan to do. Note, however, that Canada cannot in any given situation both depend on a richer and bigger power, usually the United States, in the end to do whatever is necessary and finetune the contribution of the bigger contributor by 'voting last.'

One would expect to see another kind of difference between the handling of global welfare issues and the handling of issues that directly or indirectly are believed to affect North American security. The balance between prudential consider-ations and recognition of moral obligations is not likely to be struck in quite the same way when other nations' welfare rather than one's own security is in question. Is it compassion that leads North Americans to tax themselves to alleviate human suffering in the far corners of the world, or do they recognize the inherent justice of providing aid in accordance with a rudimentary worldwide progressive income tax sys-tem, or is it a matter of prudential subsidy? The two North American countries are prime examples of what some in the Third World call the West's consumerism and of the ten-dency to form international organizations that reflect the power of producers rather than the needs of would-be consumers.[31]

However one may judge the mix of motives, there still remains the task of explaining the domestic and external pressures that govern allocation of income transfers whenever the many objectives of the transfer are not all pressing in the same direction. Perhaps because the peace dividend has historically been so large, compassionate relief has been easy for the North American countries (and for prosperous Scandinavians too), and the record is good in disaster relief and other acute emergencies. Isolationist and internationalist North Americans do not divide in the matter of relieving urgent human misery. Herbert Hoover's role in Belgian war relief and Canada's economic role in UNRRA are but two of many examples. The charitable instincts are genuine, but compassionate relief comes even more easily if there are prudential considerations pointing in the same direction. Full stomachs, the donors of agricultural surpluses genuinely believe, make for peace. What happens when alternative destinations for surplus North American grain are hungry victims of drought in the Sahiel who cannot pay for the grain and Soviet cows whose owners can is another matter.

Prudence may be another name for the ethics of responsibility, and conscience for the ethics of integrity. It may be that Canada and the United States are both trimmers but trim in ways that differ because of the unequal capabilities of one super-power and one middle power of which the people have much the same moral code. Neither government has been willing to strengthen the hands of Third World claimants for redistributive justice by actively supporting the inclusion of social and economic rights in the Universal Declaration of Human Rights. In practice, the super-power, the power of

137

self-proclaimed global responsibilities and multiple goals, has been more prone to give security considerations priority when it had to choose between 'security' and its widely trumpeted program of redemptive activism. For Canada, at least in the era of Trudeau, it has meant what he called selective targeting, a functionalist view in the Canadian tradition derived from a somewhat greater sense of limitations than those felt by his immediate predecessors.

In 1902, ten years before he was elected president, Woodrow Wilson was already saying, 'A new age is before us in which, it would seem, we must lead the world.' President Theodore Roosevelt in 1904 defined the role of the United States in only slightly less global terms when he spoke of 'our responsibility as a world power, as the dominant and order-producing nation of the Western Hemisphere.'[32] Canadians find it easier than Americans to say that they can do only so much.

A distinctively American view, though not one in which all Americans concur, is that, while violent revolution is bad, socially desirable change in some foreign country can be made to occur without such a revolution and that American power is so great that any really catastrophic failure must be the fault of some incompetent American (or, as Senator Joseph McCarthy claimed, some American traitor). Franklin Roosevelt's New Dealers proposed, according to Franz Schurmann, to make over the world after the Second World War as they had made over the United States in the 1930s. They believed, Schurmann declared, that it was their nation's peculiar mission to save the world and that if the world was not saved the fault was to be found in the United States. One who has offered eloquent testimony to the New Dealers' salvationary urge and imperial proclivities is John Holmes.

His account of the Bretton Woods Conference is an illustrative 'case.'[33]

Perhaps the functional principle can be the master criterion for determining to which demands and opportunities in the world outside North America Canadians should say 'yes' and to which they should say 'no.' To assess its utility is not easy and perhaps not possible for anyone who has not been directly involved in applying it. That Canada said 'yes' in the PJBD, in UNRRA, in FAO, in NORAD, in NATO, in international civil aviation, in peace-keeping, and in answering the duty call in Indochina is a matter of record. If the consensus in support of activism in international organizations is now less deep and less broad, functionalism seems to be a flexible enough concept to expand and contract with changing Canadian perceptions of moral duties and world conditions. The functionalist principle keeps at home the questions of just how good Canada ought to be and in what way.

What about the role of North America in promoting human freedom in a world of states? A human right is presumably one to which each individual is entitled simply by virtue of being human. If such rights are to be enforced in a world of states, who does what if a citizen's own state is the violator of his or her rights? Canadians would not look kindly at having their country hauled up before some court of world opinion to deal with allegations that the rights of native peoples were being violated. Americans do not readily acknowledge the appropriateness of being cross-examined in an international forum regarding American treatment of southern blacks, mulatto Hispanics from the Caribbean, or mestizo Hispanics from Mexico. They cannot, however, prevent others from judging them, and an important way in which North Americans can vindicate human rights is by setting such examples as they may have the resources and, increasingly, one hopes, the will to do. Meanwhile, we may expect Americans exhibiting the trait that Hans Morgenthau labelled nationalistic universalism and cautious Canadians to take different views as to what violations of human rights justify intervention by a North American state in a Third World nation's internal affairs.

Apart from setting standards by their own behavior toward their own citizens and by intervention described as humanitarian they have the possibility of legislating international goodness by tying human rights strings on foreign aid packages. Here the Congress of the United States may have played a useful role in striking a balance between 'redemptive activism' and the certified requirements of American national security.[34] The Foreign Assistance Act of 1961 provides for the withholding of foreign aid in the event of 'a consistent record of gross violations of internationally recognized human rights.' In the 1980s Congress and the president have been at odds as to what standards are to be met if El Salvador and certain other countries are not to cease receiving aid and as to who is to apply those standards.

The United States, in the oratory of its leaders, is no doubt made to sound more noble, disinterested, caring, compassionate, and responsible than any state could ever be. They declare a standard to which foreign critics can easily demonstrate American practice does not conform. Canada, with more modest pretensions, has, paradoxically, the need for reasons of national identity to take steps so as to appear noble to itself, perhaps more responsible and caring than the United States. Fortunately, its relatively low defense budgets offer Canadians the chance to match their aspirations with their performance so as to have an exceptionally humane foreign policy.[35] If Canada then appears to be the better half of North America the Good, so be it.

North Americans bulk larger on the world scene in this century than did their predecessors and perhaps larger than will their successors in future centuries. Prudential and moral considerations alike force them to pay close attention to the world outside. Prudence dictates elaborate and costly joint defense arrangements, and consciences quickened by awareness of the Third World's revolution of rising expectations dictate international income transfers which, though modest as percentages of North American GNPs, are large by standards of any earlier era.

Canada has both more and less room than the United States for disinterested normative principles to shape its foreign policy. In absolute terms the resources that Canadians can allocate to doing good are smaller than those of the Americans. Canadians have, however, retained a larger proportion of what we have called the peace dividend and may 'spend' it, within broad limits, as they choose. We have seen how those choices are affected by Canadian selectivity in promoting international distributive justice and otherwise exemplifying international goodness in accordance with the functional principle, by Canada's desire to contribute to the common defense of an area wider than North America and to the deterrence of a third world war, and by its response to rising social demands at home.[36]

Because the United States is a super-power, Americans have relatively less opportunity to pick and choose among international problems and foreign policy issues on which they will take some kind of action. Given the sense of world mission widespread among Americans, they are also more disposed to believe that they ought to make some response to every international problem. Whether the response will be enlightened or unenlightened according to the principles of prudence and morality professed by American foreign policy-makers is another matter.

Prudence and morality do not operate in separate compartments, even though it is sometimes analytically useful to write as if they do. In pluralistic societies mixed-motive actions are the rule. Liberal trade policies are good for North Americans, but pejorative characterization of them as 'free-trade imperialism' is unwarranted. Foreign aid is given more readily when it appears to be both humane and useful to prevent a Third World country from falling into what is seen as the wrong hands. Human rights violations in Poland may provide the occasion for more vigorous American diplomatic activity than any that may have occurred in Argentina or in the People's Republic of China. Canadian activism in francophone Africa serves Canadian domestic as well as foreign policy purposes. Defense arrangements to deter war in western Europe by expensive conventional rearmament lessen the threat of thermonuclear holocaust and creeping Soviet expansionism everywhere.

For North Americans the salient issues of prudence and morality all relate to the allocation of the peace dividend. North America is a fortunate continent, and the first priority of its inhabitants is to keep it that way. The prudential claims of historic entitlement, based on the fact that the first Europeans to come to North America took it away from the Indians a long time ago, have first call on resources available to support foreign policy objectives. Yet at the margins even these claims must compete with the claims of conscience of the world citizenship of Canadians and Americans. The great dilemma that the two peoples share is posed by their wish simultaneously to hold on to their favored position and to see themselves and be seen as examplary peoples doing those things that must be done if human beings everywhere are to aspire to more of the blessings North Americans now take for granted.

7 / Working together:
Predicament and opportunity

The separation of the Old World from the New and the inseparability of Canada and the United States from each other are twin geographic constants in a world of uneven change. The changes have benefited North Americans more than most other peoples and provided them with the human and material resources to play roles on the world stage dramatically larger than in the eighteenth and nineteenth centuries. They have also denied North Americans the opportunity not to play these enlarged roles.

How is North America north of the Rio Grande organized to interact with the rest of the world? What purposes do the two governments and their critics seek to promote in these interactions? These are the two main questions to which we have been seeking answers.

In the course of the nineteenth century the North American political order jelled. The British North American colonies were consolidated into a single self-governing entity, annexation by the United States ceased to be a threat or even a possibility, both countries spanned the continent, and Canada's external relations as they took shape turned out to be more North American than British imperial. They were North American in the insular era when neither the Canadian nor the American government had to do much to ensure its people's security, and they remained North American when both had to do a great deal. Their leaders discovered that they had to do much together. The consequence is that there is a de facto, though very definitely not a de jure, security union.

The relationship works one way when there is a question of North American security and the avoidance of a third world war and quite another with respect to every other aspect of foreign policy. The size of the American contribution in relation to the Canadian places the big choices in security policy in American hands. This does not rule out Canadian input, and it does leave Canadians a wide range of choice as to the level and composition of their own armed forces. Three separate but mutually reinforcing considerations may continue to keep the Canadian level low in relation to that of the United States: the United States has no choice but to defend Canada in defending itself; Canadians perceive threats to Canada's cohesiveness as the basis for high-priority allocations of the Canadian tax dollar; and like many Americans many Canadians see the American defense budget as swollen beyond need.

On the two nations' management of their purely North American affairs three points need emphasis: the absence of linkage between negotiations about North American external security and Canadian-American negotiations about anything else; the enormous volume of transborder problems, each requiring separate treatment, handled through other than diplomatic channels; and a relatively open border that lightens the burden on official diplomacy and allows free play for private international relations.

Because Canadians and Americans are less foreign to each other than they are to most other peoples their international policies would in the normal course of events run roughly parallel, but only in relation to peace and security does there appear to be a compulsion to coordinate the two countries' policies. On other matters it is sufficient that relevant policy-makers and negotiators be well-informed about the direction of each other's policies. The interests of both countries are in fact better served by avoiding coordination for its own sake; independent decisions sometimes are complementary, and they let the world see that Ottawa does not dance at the end of a string held in Washington. For Canada, playing a leading role in various kinds of multilateral diplomacy and international organizations has the added advantage of affirming Canadians' national identity to themselves. Especially in choosing policies toward the Third World the two governments are likely to differ as to the balance to be struck between prudential and moral considerations when these do not seem to point in the same direction.

The basic stability of the relationship between super-power United States and middle-power Canada is not decreed by nature. The historical momentum to maintain essentially the present pattern is very great; time, successful diplomacy, and the encrustation of private interests built up around the long-stabilized common border make that border look immovable and proper to Americans and Canadians alike. Yet Canadians, who have greater reason than Americans to worry about being masters of their own destiny, almost inevitably act on the basis of a self-disconfirming hypothesis. The best way to ensure that the American threat to Canada and what is distinctive about Canada will continue to be small and manageable is to act as if it were large and potentially unmanageable.

A small country in Europe with more than one great neighbor has historically counted on each great neighbor to protect it from the other. Canadians must find their sense of security in other ways, and they do not find it sufficient to

146

believe (as they do) that an American invasion of Canada is unimaginable (as it is). Fear of involuntary absorption has been replaced by concern to avoid informal annexation. Canada's cultural nationalism and economic protectionism need concern us in this study only in so far as they lessen the ability of the two countries to work together in the performance of tasks defined by the problems posed by the world outside North America. Whatever the effects of nationalism and protectionism, they are givens that do not seem likely to prevent essential common action.

Of more direct interest are the traditions of Canadian diplomacy – wariness, status concerns, vigilance in avoiding the creation of institutions in which Canada's veto power has been surrendered, and the pursuit of options that avoid one-on-one confrontation. There is a wide array of methods for avoiding confrontation. One is full exploitation of the possibilities of coordination by parallel action. A second, and least attractive for Canadians, is acceptance of dependence. A third, with a long history, is vigorous promotion of economic links across Canada to reduce dependence on those across the shared border. A fourth, of more historical than contemporary importance, was invocation of the British connection. A fifth is deliberate fostering of organizational and economic links with countries outside North America so as to lessen dependence on the United States. A sixth is transfer of negotiations to a multilateral forum when agreement with the United States does not come easily. Some of these can be lumped together in a basket labelled third options.

There is, however, something that may be called the fourth option. It is based on the explicit recognition that, while there is no balance of power between the two nation-states of North America, there is a political process. Neither country is a political monolith, and the fourth option for Canada is to

147

search for allies in the United States, so that the North American minority called Canada could become part of a North American majority whose policy preferences would produce parallel policies in Washington and Ottawa. The North American political process, which – though at times belatedly, grudgingly, and slowly – shifts American policy on such problems as acid rain, can also work with respect to policies toward the world as a whole.

That perhaps is what Prime Minister Trudeau had in mind when he talked of Canada's special usefulness to the United States – to hold up a mirror so that Americans can better see themselves and their own best interests.

Notes

1 Two collections of materials on regional subsystems in international politics are Louis J. Cantori and Steven L. Spiegel eds *The International Politics of Regions* (Englewood Cliffs, NJ, 1970) and Joseph S. Nye jr ed *International Regionalism* (Boston 1968). Neither contains an essay on North America. Cantori and Spiegel do, however, classify the United States and Canada as the core of a region (with a Caribbean periphery) and the two North American countries as an 'integrative system' the parts of which are less 'foreign' to each other than are the parts of other single countries (8, 382–3).

CHAPTER 1: NORTH AMERICA: TWO, THREE, OR ONE?

1 See Ellen Churchill Semple *American History and Its Geographic Condition* (Boston 1903) 230.
2 The countries of Middle America and the Caribbean have been active in inter-American and Third World politics, Castro's Cuba being the most spectacular example. In the Second World War Mexico sent (air) Squadron 201 to the Philippines, but one swallow does not make a summer.
3 See Robert A. Mackay 'The Canadian Doctrine of the Middle Powers' in Harvey L. Dyck and H. Peter Krosby eds *Empire and Nations* (Toronto 1969) 133–43; J. King Gordon ed *Canada's Role as a Middle Power* (Toronto 1966); John W. Holmes *Canada: A Middle-Aged Power* (Toronto 1976).
4 Overall power rankings seem to involve a search for 'hard' (i.e.

quantitative) data that ratify common sense. See, for example, F. Clifford German 'A Tentative Evaluation of World Power' *Journal of Conflict Resolution* IV 1 (March 1960) 138–44, in which Canada is ranked sixth (141). Data in Ray S. Cline *World Power Trends and U.S. Foreign Policy* (Boulder, Col, 1980) sharpen the distinctions between indicators of power and mobilized coercive power. The complexity of the task of power ranking is suggested by the analysis in David B. Dewitt and John J. Kirton *Canada as a Principal Power* (Toronto and New York 1983), especially chapters 1 and 5.

5 See Canada, Department of Trade and Commerce *Analysis of the Stages in the Growth of Population in Canada* (Ottawa 1935) for data on 'the early growth of population in the area now known as Canada.' The figures cited exclude the aboriginal population and are only for 'the white (including imported coloured) population' (4).

6 Geoffrey Blainey *The Tyranny of Distance* (Melbourne 1966)

7 Canada, House of Commons *Debates* (hereafter CHCD) 4 August 1944, 5909–10, quoted in Robert Mackay ed *Canadian Foreign Policy, 1945–1954* (Toronto 1970) 4–5

8 Halford J. Mackinder *Democratic Ideals and Reality* (London and New York 1919) reissued 1942 with introduction by Edward Mead Earle

9 'Rimland' is a central concept in Nicholas J. Spykman's *America's Strategy in World Politics* (New York 1942), very much as 'Heartland' is a central concept for Mackinder.

10 See Alan K. Henrikson 'The Geographical Mental Maps of American Foreign Policy Makers' *International Political Science Review* I 4 (1980) 495–530.

11 See Forrest C. Davis *The Atlantic System* (New York 1941), and J. Bartlet Brebner *The North Atlantic Triangle: The Interplay of Canada, the United States, and Great Britain* (New Haven, Conn, 1945).

12 See Alan K. Henrikson 'The Rediscovery of North America' paper given at the 74th Annual Meeting of the Organization of American Historians, Detroit, 1–4 April 1981, for a discussion of North America of the Three.

13 Lawrence H. Gipson *The Coming of the Revolution, 1763–1775* (New York 1954) 105

14 Britain's trade with Jamaica was greater than that with any two American colonies in the mid-eighteenth century. Professor Brebner judged that 'a single West Indian sugar island ... [was] thought more

valuable and more important to Britain and France than the whole of Canada'; J. Bartlet Brebner *Canada: A Modern History* (Ann Arbor, Mich, 1960) 57. How prominent the Caribbean islands must have been in the mental map of North America of observers in an earlier era is shown by the fact that so many of the volumes in Sir John W. Fortescue's *History of the British Army,* 13 volumes in 20 parts (London 1899–1930), deal extensively with operations in the Caribbean. Kenneth Maxwell has called my attention to the fact that British and French manpower losses in the Caribbean during the Napoleonic wars were on the same scale as those in Europe.

15 John and Samuel Adams quoted in Albert K. Weinberg *Manifest Destiny: A Study of Nationalist Expansionism in American History* (Baltimore 1935) 19, 23

16 John Quincy Adams in ibid 59, 61

17 Saul B. Cohen *Geography and Politics in a World Divided* (New York 1972) 124

18 See chapter 4, note 36, for examples of a vigorous expression of Canadian nationalism using the United States as a symbol of counteridentification.

19 J.C.M. Oglesby *Gringos from the Far North: Essays in the History of Canadian–Latin American Relations, 1866–1968* (Toronto 1976)

20 Henrikson 'Rediscovery of North America' 3–6

21 See Charles E. Doran 'Canada and the Reagan Administration 2: Left Hand, Right Hand' *International Journal* XXXV 1 (winter 1980–1) 236–40.

22 The phrase is quoted from the Atlantic Council's insert distributed with its *China Policy in the Next Decade* (Washington, DC, 1983).

23 Stanley W. Dziuban *Military Relations between the United States and Canada, 1939–45* (Washington, DC, 1959) 3–4

24 Charles P. Stacey *The Military Problems of Canada* (Toronto 1940) 68

25 Dziuban *Relations* 3

26 Cf Charles P. Stacey *Canada and the Age of Conflict* II *1921–1948* (Toronto 1981) 310–12, and Dziuban *Relations* 20–2.

27 Dziuban *Relations* 25

28 Ibid 26 note 80

29 George Fielding Eliot *The Ramparts We Watch: A Study of the Problems of American National Defense* (New York 1938)

30 Dziuban *Relations* 19–20

31 Alan K. Henrikson 'The Map as an Idea: The Role of Cartographic Imagery during the Second World War' *The American Cartographer* II 1 (1975) 29, quoting Henry L. Stimson and McGeorge Bundy *On Active Service in Peace and War* (New York 1947) 373

32 Dziuban *Relations* 24

CHAPTER 2: FROM PAWNS TO PLAYERS

1 Ludwig Dehio *The Precarious Balance* (New York 1962) 115

2 *Constitutional Government and Politics* rev ed (Boston 1950) 58

3 For an account of eighteenth-century international relations involving North America see Max Savelle *The Origins of American Diplomacy: The International History of Anglo-America, 1492–1763* (New York 1967). On the deteriorating relations between the British government and George III's North American subjects, see Lawrence H. Gipson *The Coming of the Revolution, 1763–1775* (New York 1954).

4 See, for example, Quincy Howe *England Expects Every American to Do His Duty* (New York 1937).

5 This particular graffito appeared in a prominent place on the walls of a Canadian university through the winter of 1971.

6 Charles P. Stacey *Canada and the Age of Conflict* II *1921–1948* (Toronto 1981) 165. Canadian skittishness about advance involvement in British war planning has a long history. See R.A. Preston *Canada and 'Imperial Defence': A Study of the Origins of the British Commonwealth's Defence Organization, 1867–1919* (Durham, NC, 1967) 313 ff.

7 See W.C. Brian Tunstall *The Commonwealth and Regional Defence* (London 1959) and Max Beloff *Imperial Sunset* I *Britain's Liberal Empire, 1897–1921* (New York 1970).

8 Quoted in Stacey *Canada and the Age of Conflict* II 165

9 Ibid 165–6

10 Felix Gilbert (*To the Farewell Address: Ideas of Early American Foreign Policy* [Princeton, NJ, 1961] 6) writes of 'the second Europe' both in terms of economic opportunity and of the opportunity to build a new society. Dehio *Balance* (viii) noted Gibbon's fear of a new barbarism overrunning Europe and the need of 10,000 ships to carry people to the 'New Europe.'

11 Forest products were important for both wealth and power. See Robert G. Albion *Forests and Sea Power* (Cambridge, Mass, 1926).

12 The British crown, after the Quebec Act of 1774, offered the prospect that Quebec could stay French and Catholic. Joining the new republic to the south did not. See pp 28–9.

13 *Disparate dyad* is the term used by the contributors to Andrew Axline et al *Continental Community?: Independence and Integration in North America* (Toronto 1974) to describe unequal neighboring states with very close relations. I have generally avoided using the term in order to emphasize the North American-ness of the Canadian-American relationship.

14 *The Origins of American Diplomacy* chapters 1 and 2

15 Quoted in ibid 28

16 Quoted in Gilbert *Farewell Address* 106

17 Ibid chapter 1

18 Gipson *Revolution* 53

19 Gilbert *Farewell Address* 13

20 Ibid 12

21 See J.F. Rippy and Angie Debo 'The Historical Background of the American Policy of Isolation' *Smith College Studies in History* IX 3 and 4 (Northampton, Mass, 1924) and J.F. Rippy *America and the Strife of Europe* (Chicago 1938) for accounts of colonial dissatisfaction with British failure to protect colonial interests.

22 Thomas Pownall *Administration of the British Colonies* (London 1774) I 40; quoted in Gilbert *Farewell Address* 108. First published in 1764, six editions had appeared by 1777. In 1780 Pownall published a pamphlet that accepted American independence as an accomplished fact and declared that 'North America is becoming a new primary planet in the system of the world' (*A Memorial Most Recently Addressed to the Sovereigns of Europe* [London 1780] 5, quoted by Gilbert *Farewell Address* 109).

23 Gilbert *Farewell Address* 30 and Vincent T. Harlow *The Founding of the Second British Empire 1763–1793* I (London 1952) 162 note 27. For the pro-Guadeloupe rationale see ibid I 162ff.

24 Perhaps because of its long-term relevance to the roles Canada and the United States play in the world today, I have stressed the importance of the western lands as a cause of and prize in the American Revolution. Gipson's *Revolution,* in its balanced and

judicious interpretation of events after 1763 that brought the
colonial leaders to the point of rebellion, shows how a clash of
economic interest became transformed into a struggle over
constitutional principles.

25 Ibid 111

26 Dehio *Balance* 123

27 My italics; text of the Articles of Peace reprinted in Samuel F. Bemis
The Diplomacy of the American Revolution rev ed (Bloomington, Ind,
1956) 259–64. The Articles of Peace were called 'preliminary and
conditional' because the Americans had promised the French not to
make a separate peace. The complicated parallel negotiations in
Paris in 1782 between Britain and the as-yet-unrecognized United
States and between Britain and France are recounted in detail and
shrewdly interpreted in Bemis's definitive study (chapters 13–18).

28 Bemis *Diplomacy of the American Revolution* 196

29 Article 3, quoted in J. Bartlet Brebner *Canada: A Modern History*
(Ann Arbor, Mich, 1960) 116. In 1928 it was finally decided by the
US Supreme Court in *U.S.* vs. *Karnuth* that the Treaty of Ghent in
1815 had superseded Jay's Treaty (ibid 445). R.W. Van Alstyne in
The Rising American Empire points out that Lord Shelburne's offer
of reciprocal American and Canadian trade and travel rights
through the interior of North America meant little to the Americans
in the 1780s and 1790s. For a discussion of the British argument
about North America, Shelburne's policy during the American
peace negotiations, and the question of trade reciprocity, see Harlow
The Founding of the Second British Empire chapters 5, 6, and 9. For
details of the negotiations, especially on the American side, see
Bemis *Diplomacy of the American Revolution* chapters 13–18.

30 Brebner *Canada* 114

31 Adrienne Koch and William Peden *The Life and Selected Writings of
Thomas Jefferson* (New York 1944) 656. Jefferson was by no means
the first to foresee that the majority of English-speaking peoples
would one day be in North America. Although he did not foresee
American independence, Adam Smith wrote in *The Wealth of
Nations* (1776): 'Such has hitherto been the rapid progress of that
country in wealth, population and improvement that in the course of
little more than a century, perhaps, the produce of American might
exceed that of English taxation. The seat of the Empire would then
naturally remove itself to that part of the Empire which contributed

most to the general defence and support of the whole'; quoted in Vincent T. Harlow *Founding of the Second British Empire* (London 1952) 200.

32 G.K. Chesterton *The Victorian Age in Literature* (New York 1913, reprinted Notre Dame, Ind, 1962) 17–18

33 Charles P. Stacey 'The Myth of the Unguarded Frontier, 1815–1871' *American Historical Review* LVI (1950) 1–18; Richard A. Preston *The Defence of the Undefended Border: Planning for War in North America, 1867–1939* (Montreal 1977)

34 The quoted phrase is from Bemis *Diplomacy of the American Revolution* 133.

35 Preston *Defence* 21

36 These are but two of a group of similar grandiloquent statements brought together in Albert K. Weinberg *Manifest Destiny: A Study of Nationalist Expansionism in American History* (Baltimore 1935) 53–61. The 'natural' unity of two-state North America continued to be asserted long after Americans had ceased to assert any right of annexation. See Goldwin Smith *Canada and the Canadian Question* (London and New York 1891), and Samuel E. Moffett *The Americanization of Canada* (New York 1907, reissued Toronto 1977).

37 Southern senators voted in 1854 to ratify the Marcy-Elgin Treaty providing for trade reciprocity with Canada to head off pressure for the United States to annex free-soil Canada; Samuel F. Bemis *A Diplomatic History of the United States* 3rd edn (New York 1950) 301. It was Professor Bemis's judgment that there has never been a time when a president and the two houses of Congress would all have agreed to voluntary annexation.

38 Bemis *Diplomatic History* 381–2; J. Bartlet Brebner *The North Atlantic Triangle: The Interplay of Canada, the United States, and Great Britain* (New Haven, Conn, 1960) 163–4; 169–70

39 Brebner *North Atlantic Triangle* 165 (for the Seward statement), 170 (on the Taylor Bill). On the purchase of Alaska and its bearing on the annexation question see Bemis *Diplomatic History* 397–9. Lord Stanley, then Britain's foreign secretary, judged that Seward, like Sumner, believed that the purchase of Alaska provided a short-cut route to the annexation of Canada; Kenneth Bourne *Britain and the Balance of Power in North America, 1815–1908* (London 1967) 302.

40 Seward's general posture may be deduced from the report of Lord Lyons, then the minister in Washington, that the defenselessness of

155

Canada would in Seward's view make Britain eat 'any amount of dirt'; Bourne *Balance* 311.

41 Brebner *North Atlantic Triangle* 169

42 Quoted in Stacey *Canada and the Age of Conflict* I *1867–1921* (Toronto 1977) 2

43 See Seymour M. Lipset *The First New Nation: The United States in Historical and Comparative Perspective* (New York 1963).

44 Dehio (*Balance* 175) declares that it 'was forecast as a probability at the time' that the United States was 'a world power in the making.'

45 Bemis *Diplomacy of the American Revolution* 12

46 Quoted in Alan K. Henrikson 'The Rediscovery of North America' paper given at the 74th Annual Meeting of the Organization of American Historians, 1–4 April 1981, 48, and in Norman Graebner *Ideas and Diplomacy: Readings in the Intellectual Tradition of American Foreign Policy* (New York 1964) 78

47 See Walter Lippmann *U.S. Foreign Policy: Shield of the Republic* (New York 1943) and Samuel F. Bemis 'Walter Lippmann on U.S. Foreign Policy' *Hispanic-American Historical Review* (November 1983) 664–7. The Lippmann thesis is further brought into question by Kenneth Bourne's *Britain and the Balance of Power in North America.*

CHAPTER 3: BRITISH EMPIRE AND INSULAR NORTH AMERICA

1 See Kenneth Bourne *Britain and the Balance of Power in North America, 1815–1908* (London 1967) 146.

2 In support of this conclusion Bourne quotes several paragraphs from Sir George Murray's Memorandum about the Defence of Canada, 8 September 1845 (ibid 147–8).

3 R.A. Preston *Canada and 'Imperial Defense': A Study of the Origins of the British Commonwealth's Defense Organization, 1867–1919* (Durham, NC, 1967) 2–3, citing 1851 correspondence from the secretary of state for war and the colonies, Henry Earl Grey, to Lord Elgin, Canada's governor

4 William Roger Louis *Imperialism at Bay* (New York 1978) vii–viii, quoting Taylor's reply to a query about 'maintenance of the Empire' as a British war aim in the Second World War

5 The American Civil War had briefly interrupted and reversed the process of bringing British garrisons home, but the prompt demobilization of the Northern armies after General Robert E. Lee's surrender at Appomatox in April 1865 permitted its resumption and completion. See Preston *Canada and 'Imperial Defense'* 34–5.

6 As late as the 1920s at least one Canadian student of international affairs was still stressing the importance of the British connection so as to overcome 'the strategic weakness of the frontiers with the United States.' See H.A. Smith's appendix on Canada's strategic position in Percy E. Corbett and H.A. Smith *Canada and World Politics: A Study of the Constitutional and International Relations of the British Empire* (London 1928). Of course, there were many non-military reasons why that connection might have been helpful to Canada in its dealings with the United States.

7 'Decline of Anglo-American hostility' is the unifying theme of Kenneth Bourne's *Britain and the Balance of Power in North America,* an absorbing examination of 'the problems raised by thinking about and planning for the possibility of a future war with the United States' (vii).

8 *Satellite* has replaced *pawn* as the more common term in expressions of concern about the subordination of Canada's to American interests. See, for example, Kenneth McNaught 'From Colony to Satellite' in Stephen Clarkson ed *An Independent Foreign Policy for Canada?* (Toronto 1968) 177–83.

9 For matters discussed in this paragraph see Paul M. Kennedy *The Rise of Anglo-German Antagonism, 1860–1914* (London 1980).

10 The theme developed by Lionel Gelber in his *Rise of Anglo-American Friendship* (London and New York 1938) has been further elaborated in a number of monographs, the most important of which are listed by Bourne *Britain and the Balance of Power in North America* vii–viii.

11 Richard A. Preston *The Defence of the Undefended Border: Planning for War in North America, 1867–1919* (Montreal 1977) 4

12 Ibid 86

13 Sir Wilfrid Laurier used the 'inaccessibility' argument in 1897 to argue that the Royal Navy was not as important for Canada as for the other parts of the empire; conflicts with the United States he described as family problems, 'nothing serious.' Sir John A.

Macdonald had earlier gone further, arguing that it was dangerous for Canada to contribute to Britain's Navy because it would scare the United States; Preston *Canada and 'Imperial Defence'* 113, 187.

14 Charles P. Stacey *Canada and the Age of Conflict* I *1867–1921* (Toronto 1977) 75. The photograph is reproduced in this volume.

15 Ibid 75–7. Cf Max Beloff *Imperial Sunset* I *Britain's Liberal Empire, 1897–1921* (New York 1970) chapter 3, 'The Weary Titan.'

16 Preston *Canada and 'Imperial Defense'* 502. See J.D.B. Miller *Richard Jebb and The Problem of Empire* (London 1956) for a description of Jebb's 'autonomist' vision of the empire's future as opposed to the 'centralist' vision of Lionel Curtis and the Round Table advocates of imperial federation. Jebb's vision of a partnership or alliance among Britain and the self-governing colonies corresponds closely to the Commonwealth realized after 1945. On the question of Canadian participation in early meetings of the Committee of Imperial Defence, see Preston *Canada and 'Imperial Defense'* 313ff.

17 Quoted in Joseph Levitt *A Vision beyond Reach: A Century of Images of Canadian Destiny* (Ottawa 1982) 11

18 Charles P. Stacey *Canada and the Age of Conflict* II *1921–48* (Toronto 1981) 13

19 John W. Holmes *The Shaping of Peace: Canada and the Search for World Order, 1943–1957* I (Toronto 1979) 5

20 Stacey *Canada and the Age of Conflict* II 132–3

21 See Holmes *Shaping of Peace* I 247 and 250.

22 The Christie statement is quoted in Stacey *Canada and the Age of Conflict* I 337. Meighen's statement was made in London, 22 June 1921, at the conference of prime ministers (ibid 339).

23 J. Bartlet Brebner *Canada: A Modern History* (Ann Arbor, Mich, 1960) 418

24 The Australian prime minister, William Morris (Billy) Hughes, declared that the Canadian defense budget showed what 'it means to have a great neighbour like America as its neighbour, under whose wing the Dominion of Canada can nestle in safety'; Stacey *Canada in the Age of Conflict* I 343.

25 The huge Canadian investment in building a transcontinental railroad system and other elements in the infrastructure of a new country was frequently cited by Canadian leaders as an explanation

for low defense budgets and Canadian inability to contribute to imperial defense.

26 'The Round World and the Winning of the Peace' *Foreign Affairs* XXI 4 (July 1943) 595–605

27 In addition to Nicholas J. Spykman's *America's Strategy in World Politics* (New York 1942), see also his posthumous *Geography of the Peace* (New York 1944).

28 Western hemisphere defense would not in Spykman's view assure North America's security; isolationism with an expanded territorial base was still isolationism and, once insularity had been lost, inappropriate. His concern to establish this proposition led him to devote almost half of *America's Strategy* to material relating to Latin America and hemisphere defense. In the dark days of 1940 after the fall of France an Axis victory over Britain and France did not seem an implausible contingency, and American interest in the Caribbean and Latin America suddenly mushroomed. In the so-called 'Rainbow' plans of the American war planners, preparing for the defense of the Caribbean and of South America down to the hump of Brazil was of great importance. In a way, that planning process complemented the political-military arrangements involving the United States, Canada, and Newfoundland made following the Ogdensburg declaration.

29 Quoted in John W. Holmes *The Shaping of Peace: Canada and the Search for World Order, 1943–57* II (Toronto 1982) 104

CHAPTER 4: THE NORTH AMERICAN-NESS OF NORTH AMERICA

1 Joseph Levitt quotes O.D. Skelton, in the interwar period King's closest foreign policy adviser, as declaring in 1909 that American 'problems and their state of advance are more nearly like ours' than, presumably, like Britain's and Europe's; *A Vision beyond Reach: A Century of Images of Canadian Destiny* (Ottawa 1982) 48.

2 See A.R.M. Lower *Canada: Nation and Neighbour* (Toronto 1952) and the characterization of Professor Lower's views in Levitt *A Vision* chapter 8.

3 'Independent but not foreign' was the way that James T. Shotwell, the general editor of the Carnegie Endowment for International

Peace series on Canadian-American relations, described each country in relation to the other.

4 Peyton V. Lyon's testimony on 6 March 1975, Senate of Canada, *Proceedings* of the Standing Senate Committee on Foreign Affairs, First Session, Thirtieth Parliament, 1974–5, Issue No. 9, 7

5 Quoted in Albert K. Weinberg *Manifest Destiny: A Study of Nationalist Expansionism in American History* (Baltimore 1935) 39

6 Most Americans who then thought about it at all would have preferred to see the Canada of that day brought into the new American union.

7 Quoted in Weinberg *Manifest Destiny* 1

8 Both the Massey and the Harding quotations are to be found in ibid 379.

9 Claude T. Bissell 'A Common Ancestry: Literature in Australia and Canada' *University of Toronto Quarterly* XXV (1956) 131–42

10 S. M. Lipset 'Anglo-American Society' *International Encyclopedia of the Social Sciences* 1 (New York 1968) 300

11 In the conference preceding publication of the symposium volume edited by Dick Harrison, *Crossing Frontiers: Papers on American and Canadian Literature* (Edmonton, Alta, 1979), one participant observed: 'In this experiment in comparative cultural analysis, it was interesting to see that the American scholars were concerned with similarities and the Canadian scholars with differences'; Arnold E. Davidson's review of *Crossing Frontiers* in *American Review of Canadian Studies* (autumn 1980) 112.

12 John W. Holmes *The Shaping of Peace: Canada and the Search for World Order, 1943–57* 1 (Toronto 1979) 298

13 Speech at Notre Dame University, 16 May 1982

14 On Anglo-American voluntarism versus continental necessity see Arnold Wolfers 'Political Theory and International Relations' in Arnold Wolfers and Laurence Martin eds *The Anglo-American Tradition in Foreign Affairs* (New Haven, Conn, 1956) ix–xxvii, reprinted in Wolfers *Discord and Collaboration* (Baltimore, Md, 1962) 233–51. See also William T.R. Fox *The American Study of International Relations* (Columbia, SC, 1967).

15 Quoted in Weinberg *Manifest Destiny* 468. On the historic polarity between good, natural, unspoiled America and bad, artificial, corrupt Europe, see Daniel Boorstin *America and the Image of Europe* (Gloucester, Mass, 1960) 19–42.

16 See Donald M. Page 'Canada as the Exponent of American Idealism' *American Review of Canadian Studies* III 2 (autumn 1973) 31–46.

17 Quoted in James Eayrs *In Defence of Canada* I *From the Great War to the Great Depression* (Toronto 1964) 4

18 Weinberg *Manifest Destiny* 227

19 Eayrs *In Defence of Canada* I 5

20 Page 'Exponent' 31

21 CHCD, 1936, I, 97, quoted in James Eayrs *In Defence of Canada* II *Appeasement and Rearmament* (Toronto 1965) 29

22 James A. Macdonald *The North American Idea* (Toronto 1917)

23 Quoted in Levitt *A Vision* 75

24 Page 'Exponent' 34

25 Ibid 37

26 Eayrs *In Defence of Canada* I 5

27 Carl C. Berger 'Internationalism, Continentalism, and the Writing of History: Comments on the Carnegie Series on the Relations of Canada and the United States' in Richard A. Preston ed *The Influence of the United States on Canadian Development: Eleven Case Studies* (Durham, NC, 1972) 32–54

28 See Michael F. Scheuer 'Peter Buell Porter and the Development of the Joint Commission Approach to Diplomacy in the North Atlantic Triangle' *American Review of Canadian Studies* XII 1 (spring 1982) 65–73.

29 Andrew Axline et al *Continental Community?: Independence and Integration in North America* (Toronto 1974) especially chapters 3 and 4

30 The Soviet Union and the Chinese People's Republic have a long common frontier in Asia, but much of it is sparsely populated and the power centers of the two countries are far apart.

31 A.E. Gotlieb 'Power and Vulnerability: Canadian and American Perspectives on International Affairs' an address given to the Harvard University Seminar on Canada-U.S.A. Relations on 15 February 1978, when he was under-secretary of state for external affairs (mimeographed, Ottawa 1978)

32 Erwin Raisz *Atlas of Global Geography* (New York 1944)

33 Berger 'Internationalism' 34. See also Marcus Lee Hansen *The Mingling of the Canadian and American Peoples* (New Haven 1940); in the preface (viii) James T. Shotwell describes this mingling as 'the

161

largest single reciprocity in international migration in history.' This is one important, though not the only, reason why social scientists in their efforts to measure cohesion, communication, interaction, and cooperation find many Canadians and Americans less 'foreign' to each other than they do some peoples living within the same country. See Louis J. Cantori and Steven L. Spiegel *The International Politics of Regions* (Englewood Cliffs, NJ, 1970) 383.

34 The emergence of the concept of the exclusive economic zone extending 200 miles outward from each country's coast has created a whole new set of boundary problems in three widely separated areas – the Georges Bank, the Strait of Juan de Fuca, and the Beaufort Sea.

35 There will continue to be difficulties and frictions that arise from the efforts of one of the governments, more often the Canadian, to control the flow of people, goods, ideas, capital, etc between the two countries. In this connection, the case for cultural and intellectual nationalism would seem to be stronger than the case for economic nationalism. See Claude T. Bissell's essay in Richard H. Leach ed *Contemporary Canada* (Durham, NC, 1967) 190.

36 For example, James M. Minifie *Peacemaker or Powder Monkey: Canada's Role in a Revolutionary World* (Toronto 1960), Kari Levitt *Silent Surrender* (Toronto 1970), Ian Lumsden ed *Close the 49th Parallel, Etc.: The Americanization of Canada* (Toronto 1970), and Kenneth McNaught 'From Colony to Satellite' in Stephen Clarkson ed *An Independent Foreign Policy for Canada?* (Toronto 1968)

CHAPTER 5: LIMITED PARTNERSHIP FOR PEACE AND SECURITY

1 The self-satisfaction in the inter-war period of North Americans celebrating the long unbroken peace along the Canadian-American border is reflected in the naming of the Peace Bridge across the Niagara River between Buffalo and Fort Erie and in the establishment of a 'peace garden' in the form of an international park straddling the North Dakota–Saskatchewan border.

2 The parochial success of North Americans in keeping the peace with each other does not by itself exorcise the threat of war anywhere else in the world. One aspect of the claims of special virtue for the way Canadians and Americans have kept the peace in North America deserves further comment. 'Peace,' it was often said, was the

consequence of having proper mechanisms and signing proper treaties for 'adjusting' international differences. Peace in North America and war in Europe were not, however, to be explained by the presence of machinery for cranking out peace, justice, and order on one side of the Atlantic and the absence of such machinery on the other.

'Adjusting' suggests that real clashes of interest can be settled by technical, apolitical means. Thus, Mackenzie King, a politician with a pre–First World War background in industrial relations, could refer, as we have already noted (p 67), to the International Joint Commission set up by the United States and Canada in 1909 as a 'new world answer to old world queries as to the most effective methods of adjusting international differences.' Nicholas Mansergh may have had this sort of observation in mind when he wrote of 'the Canadians' platitudinous and at time [sic] irrelevant advice on how to settle their problems by the methods of conciliation and arbitration'; *Survey of Commonwealth Affairs: Problems of External Policy, 1931–39* (London 1952) 86; quoted in Michael F. Scheuer 'Peter Buell Porter and the Development of the Joint Commission Approach to Diplomacy in the North Atlantic Triangle' *American Review of Canadian Studies* XII 1 (spring 1982) 65.

3 Canada's active role in security arrangements for North America's Arctic frontier, for the North Atlantic, and for western Europe has no parallel in the Pacific or in eastern Asia. The Americans have filled that vacuum.

4 The chill is nowhere more chillingly described than in Stephen Clarkson's *Canada and the Reagan Challenge* (Toronto 1983). The challenge is not as menacing as in the first years after the American Civil War or as rude as that of Theodore Roosevelt in the Alaskan-Canadian boundary dispute. The Canadian response has not been as strong as in 1911, when a storm in Canadian-American economic relations turned the government of Sir Wilfrid Laurier out of office. Neither has the challenge been as abrupt as in the case of the 'Nixon shock' of 1971. A new ice age in Canadian-American relations did not close in in the early 1980s.

As Charles F. Doran has convincingly shown in *Forgotten Partnership: U.S.-Canadian Relations Today* (Baltimore 1984), a significant change in the relationship, reflecting policy shifts in both Washington and Ottawa, did occur in the 1970s. Not only, he

163

declares, is partnership forgotten, but the decade before President Reagan took office had already seen the demise of the two countries' special relationship (20ff). My own apparently more optimistic judgment is not necessarily inconsistent with his. He says the bottle is half-empty; I say it is half-full. His focus is on the last and the next decades. My time horizon is longer.

5 For a discussion of Canada's 'new found acceptance of concentrating on resource-related products which have a comparative advantage' see Keith Hay in *International Perspectives* (July–August 1981) 16. The acceptance is 'new found' because it runs counter to a common Canadian dislike of an economic role for Canadians as 'hewers of wood and drawers of water.'

6 Peyton Lyon's statement to the Canadian Senate's Standing Committee on Foreign Affairs, 6 March 1975, is a good and succinct description of the Canadian-American special relationship. He discussed it in structural terms (high interaction and power disparity), in procedural terms (easy communication, few suspicions, quiet diplomacy, assumption of basic compatibility of interests, absence of threats), and in terms of preferential treatment for Canada. On the high degree of informal economic integration see William Diebold jr *The United States and the Industrial World: American Foreign Economic Policy in the 1970s* (New York 1972) chapter 4, 'Canada: A Special Relation.'

7 It would be hard to find an American who thought Canadians ought to agree to be Americans though not difficult to find Americans who think Canadians would be better off if Canada did join the United States. It would be even harder to find a Canadian who thought that Canada ought to annex the United States, a possibility to which President Harding humorously referred in his 1923 Vancouver speech. 'Do not,' said Harding to his Canadian audience, 'encourage any enterprise looking to Canada's annexation of the United States. You are one of the most capable governing peoples of the world, but I entreat you for your own sake to think twice before undertaking management of the territory between the Great Lakes and the Rio Grande'; quoted in Albert K. Weinberg *Manifest Destiny: A Study of Nationalist Expansionism in American History* (Baltimore 1935) 379.

8 Jacob Viner, in writing about world federation a few months after the dropping of atom bombs on Hiroshima and Nagasaki, argued that the United States and the Soviet Union were too big to enter

such a federation and, if there were to be one, each of the Big Two would have to be broken up for the federation to succeed; Jacob Viner 'The Implications of the Atomic Bomb for International Relations' *Proceedings* of the American Philosophical Society XL 1 (29 January 1946) 53ff, especially 56.

9 The National Energy Program (NEP) has sometimes been seen as a power play in a Canadian federal-provincial struggle. Its authors were not maliciously anti-American but simply heedless of its consequences for Canadian-American relations. The case may be different for some Canadians not in the government who enthusiastically applauded the NEP. See Clarkson *Canada and the Reagan Challenge* 79.

10 On 'structural violence' and informal imperialism generally see Johan Galtung 'Violence, Peace, and Peace Research' *Journal of Peace Research* VI 3 (1969) 167–91, and Galtung 'A Structural Theory of Imperialism' ibid VIII 2 (1971) 81–117. For BINGOs, IGOs, etc, see the latter article, 91.

11 The pattern of American investment resulting in the celebrated branch-plant phenomenon is sometimes cited as evidence of American neocolonialism or informal, i.e. nongovernmental, imperialism. In fact, it is more the product of Canadian than of American policy; Canadian protectionism and imperial preferences hindered American manufacturers from entering the Canadian market unless they risked their capital, built factories, and hired a workforce in Canada. Canada's huge financial institutions have by their lending practices been reshaping the downtown areas of many American cities and financing merger maneuvers that many think use capital that could be invested in socially more useful ways.

12 Peyton V. Lyon and Brian W. Tomlin in their discussion of transnational informal integration (*Canada as an International Actor* [Toronto 1979] 109–11) reported that 71 per cent of Canadian union members belonged to international unions.

13 'Continentalism' is a code-word some Canadian nationalists use to attack 'open border' policies that they see as serving American but not Canadian interests. They see such policies as threatening Canada's sense of identity, its control over its own fate, and perhaps even its survival. George Grant in his *Lament for a Nation* (Toronto 1965) portrays the economic interests of Canada's business and financial élites as tied to the continental economy and takes a

165

gloomy view of Canada's future.

14 Two presentations at the conference of the Association for Canadian
Studies in the United States (ACSUS) in Rockport, Maine, 30
September 1983, suggest that neither the diagnosis nor the
prescription for the problem of Canadian civic education is simple.
Don Page reported evidence that 'non-media variables,' e.g., the
teaching of Canadian history to Canadians, may be more
fundamental determinants of Canadian perspectives than television
broadcasts from over the border. In the discussion led by Victor
Howard an asymmetry in foreign news was reported: Canadian
Press covers Canada for the American press, but Associated Press
covers the world for the Canadian press.

15 The contrast is in one respect sharp between the openness of North
America today and that of the British Commonwealth of imperial
preferences days and the EEC of the present era. Walls have not been
built up around North America as holes have been punched in the
wall that divides it.

16 Not since the Alaskan-Canadian boundary dispute finally was
settled in 1903 has an American government threatened to use the
massive coercive power at its disposal in its relations with Canada.
Theodore Roosevelt's blunt language, his order of military
reinforcements into the disputed area, and his intimidating
communications while the 'ostensible arbitration' was in progress
seem to have been gratuitous given the strength of the American
legal position. 'Ostensible' and 'so-called' are the adjectives Samuel
F. Bemis used to characterize the 'arbitration' by which this dispute
was settled; *A Diplomatic History of the United States* 3rd edn (New
York 1950) 426 and 428. There are earlier examples of heavyhanded
American efforts to intimidate, at least one of which backfired. The
abrupt termination of the reciprocity treaty in 1865–6, as we saw in
chapter 2, provided an additional stimulus to Confederation.

17 On environmental relations see Annette Baker Fox 'Environmental
Issues: Canada and the United States' in Willis C. Armstrong,
Louise S. Armstrong, and Francis O. Wilcox eds *Canada and the
United States: Dependence and Divergence* (Cambridge, Mass, 1982)
189–220.

18 To avoid the appearance of being a bad neighbour the Trudeau
government modified in certain details the provisions for

implementing the NEP and the Foreign Investment Review Act so as to meet specific criticisms by American officials. They did not retreat on general principles.

19 For a detailed discussion see David Leyton-Brown 'The Multinational Enterprise and Conflict in Canadian-American Relations' in Annette Baker Fox, Alfred O. Hero, and Joseph Nye eds *Canada and the United States: Transnational and Transgovernmental Relations* (New York 1975); previously published as symposium issue of *International Organization* (autumn 1974). For a general discussion of how the mechanism has worked see Annette Baker Fox *The Politics of Attraction: Four Middle Powers and the United States* (New York 1977) 170–1, 174, 178–9, and 188–9.

20 David B. Dewitt and John J. Kirton *Canada as a Principal Power* (Toronto and New York 1983), however, suggest that there may be opportunities for Canadian diplomacy to try to gain by linking issues (80).

21 John W. Holmes *The Shaping of Peace: Canada and the Search for World Order, 1943–57* II (Toronto 1982) 339–42

22 Clarkson *Canada and the Reagan Challenge* 39

23 Peter Dobell has pointed out a parallel that may not be accidental; *Canada's Search for New Roles: Foreign Policy in the Trudeau Era* (London 1972) 58. The Trudeau foreign policy review of 1970 contained no overall assessment of Canadian policy toward the United States. This glaring omission was matched by the failure of President Nixon in either of his 'State of the World' statements (1971 and 1972) to include a section dealing with Canada. One explanation may be that the heterogeneity and quasi-domestic character of intra–North American Canadian-American relations and the pervasiveness of the other country's participation in the extra–North American international relations of each make such overall assessments impossible. John Holmes has judged 'the American government machine ... too incoherent to formulate a co-ordinated Canadian policy'; Holmes *Life with Uncle: The Canadian-American Relationship* (Toronto 1981) 55. This assumes both that machinery is the root cause of incoherent policies and that coherence is generally to be desired. Of course, if Professor Holmes is referring to malcoordination rather than to noncoordination, to a government so organized that it cannot make a clear commitment and fulfill it

rather than to one organized so as to ensure ad hoc handling of diverse and numerous issues, his statement would be more a constitutional criticism than a political judgment.

24 Henrikson 'The Geographical Mental Maps of American Foreign Policy Makers' *International Political Science Review* 1 4 (1980) 497, citing Daniel J. Boorstin *The Exploring Spirit: America and the World, Then and Now* (New York 1976) 76. Boorstin relates American 'hyperopia' to television and radio, which make the distant seem close. A deeper problem may be the American tendency not to see Canada as 'foreign' and therefore not to think about it in terms of foreign relations and world politics.

25 See William R. Willoughby *The St. Lawrence Seaway* (Toronto 1979).

26 John W. Holmes *The Shaping of Peace: Canada and the Search for World Order, 1943–57* 1 (Toronto 1979) 45

27 Canadian human and material resources are described by John Holmes as 'just enough to get us involved in every U.S. adventure or screw up every decision by Washington on which the peace of the world may depend'; *Life with Uncle* 87.

28 Charles Ritchie *Diplomatic Passport* (Toronto 1981) 56

29 For example, during the war in Korea Canadians unsuccessfully tried to dissuade the Americans from pushing north of the thirty-eighth parallel. See the exhaustive treatment of Canadian diplomacy regarding American leadership in Denis Stairs *The Diplomacy of Constraint: Canada, the Korean War, and the United States* (Toronto 1974). On pressing the Canadian view pragmatically with more powerful allies see Peyton V. Lyon *The Policy Question: A Critical Appraisal of Canada's Role in World Affairs* (Toronto 1963) chapter 5, especially 83–4.

30 On the rationality of weapons-acquisition decisions for anti-submarine warfare, given the premises of Prime Minister Trudeau's foreign and defense policies, see Michael Tucker *Canadian Foreign Policy: Contemporary Issues and Themes* (Toronto 1980) chapter 5.

31 The letter appeared in leading newspapers throughout Canada.

32 Pearson's diary entry of 30 April 1940; *Mike, The Memoirs of the Right Honourable Lester B. Pearson* 1 *1897–1948* (Toronto 1972) 168

33 Eayrs *In Defence of Canada* 1 *From the Great War to the Great Depression* (Toronto 1964) 14

34 On the Canadian government's reactions at the time of the Cuban

missile crisis see Robert Reford *Canada and Three Crises* (Toronto 1968) 147ff; Peyton V. Lyon *Canada in World Affairs, 1961–1963* (Toronto 1968) 32–51; and Jocelyn Ghent 'Canada, the United States and the Cuban Missile Crisis' *Pacific Historical Review* XLVIII (March 1979) 159–84.

35 Charles P. Stacey *Canada and the Age of Conflict* II *1921–48* (Toronto 1981) 160

36 William T.R. Fox, 'The Super-Powers at San Francisco' *Review of Politics* VIII 1 (January 1946) 122–3 and 126–7

37 Holmes *Shaping of Peace* I 160

38 Ibid 145

39 Lester Pearson's comment on the Halifax speech was that 'acting in unison as separate states is one thing; acting as a unit is another.' This comment is as relevant to Canadian-American relations for the foreseeable future as it once was to Anglo-Canadian relations. After the San Francisco Conference the South African prime minister, Jan Christian Smuts, in a speech in Ottawa described the provision for 'collective self-defense' in article 51 of the UN Charter as the most important change in the Dumbarton Oaks Proposals made at the conference. He seems to have understood that the problem was not for the Commonwealth to gain parity with the United States, but for the United States and the independent members of the Commonwealth working together to underwrite the post-1945 order.

On the significance of article 51 more generally and of article 44, which met the Canadian demand that a country contributing armed forces should share in Security Council decisions regarding their employment, see William T.R. Fox 'Collective Enforcement of Peace and Security' *American Political Science Review* XXXIX 5 (October 1945) 970–81.

40 Martin Wight referred to the League of Nations as 'none other than the ghost of the Pax Britannica'; 'Western Values in International Relations' in Herbert Butterfield and Martin Wight eds *Diplomatic Investigations* (London 1966) 121.

41 Gerald Wright in his 'Canada and the Reagan Administration' (*International Journal* [Winter 1980–1] 228–9) refers to the open access the Canadian ambassador had to then vice-president Mondale and to the liberal use of the Washington-Ottawa 'hot line' during the period in which decisions were being taken about a grain

169

embargo after the Soviet invasion of Afghanistan.

42 The distinction between the 'civic order' of informal groups and the 'political order' of formal public authorities and institutions is made by Harold D. Lasswell *A Pre-View of Policy Sciences* (New York 1971) 1–2.

43 John Holmes's worry (*Life with Uncle* 94) that Canadians may be 'hypnotized into seeing ourselves too exclusively as North American' could refer both to intimate interaction between opposite numbers at policy-making levels and to the flourishing North American 'civic order' in which Canadian-ness might be diluted in the decision and opinion processes of non-official transnational groups. His subsequent description of world culture and of the consequent threat to Canada of intellectual annexation (110) strengthens this impression.

44 Prime Minister Trudeau, in his speech at Notre Dame University, 16 May 1982, referred to the 'super-responsibility' of the super-power.

45 Ibid. In 1982 what the Canadian looking glass would have helped the Americans to see was their government's position about 'survivability' and 'demonstration explosions' during a crisis involving the possible use of nuclear weapons. Tucker describes 'Trudeauvian internationalism' in terms of Canada being a 'mentor state' but more as a teacher of Third World countries than of the United States (*Canadian Foreign Policy* 10ff). Lyon (*The Policy Question* 89) refers to the prestige and influence Canada acquires by setting an example of being indifferent to prestige and influence.

46 Ritchie *Diplomatic Passport* 164

47 See Lester B. Pearson *Mike: The Memoirs of the Right Honourable Lester B. Pearson* III *1957–68* (Toronto 1975) 147–58. A particularly colorful account is given in Lawrence Martin *The Presidents and the Prime Ministers* (Toronto 1982) 223–8.

48 See Dobell *Canada's Search* 79–82; U.S. Department of State *Bulletin* 11 May 1970; A.E. Gotlieb and C. Dalfen 'National Jurisdiction and International Responsibility: New Canadian Approaches to International Law' *American Journal of International Law* LXVII (April 1973); D.M. McRae 'Arctic Waters and Canadian Sovereignty' *International Journal* 38 (summer 1983) 476–92; and Jan Schneider *World Public Order of the Environment: Towards an International Ecological Law and Organization* (Toronto 1979). The final draft of the law-of-the-sea convention legitimized a 200-mile

exclusive economic zone, which in effect represented an expansion of Canada's earlier claim to exclusive fishery zones off parts of its coast. A major achievement of the Canadian government in the multilateral negotiations was recognition of Canada's claim to protect waters subject to pollution. Article 234 provides that 'coastal states have the right to adopt and enforce non-discriminatory laws and regulations for the prevention, reduction and control of marine pollution from vessels in ice-covered areas within the limits of the exclusive economic zone.'

The United States has also sometimes mobilized 'outside' countervailing pressure. It cited GATT rules in its partly successful effort to ease the impact of Canada's Foreign Investment Review Act on adversely affected Americans. See G.C. Hufbauer and A.J. Samet 'Investment Relations between Canada and the United States' in Armstrong et al *Canada and the United States: Dependence and Divergence* 111–13.

49 *Shaping of Peace* II 248
50 Franz Schurmann *The Logic of World Power* (New York 1974) 362–3. He says that in the 1960s the Chinese were under no illusion that Canada was a 'country seeking independence' but saw it as a 'kind of proxy for America' and dealings with Canada as 'a way ... of getting a sense of what a future direct relationship with America might be.'
51 John Halstead, a former Canadian permanent representative at NATO, has written, 'As a North American country which is not a great power and which shares perceptions and interests with Europe as well as with the United States, Canada has an important bridging role to play in NATO, not as a mediator (that is not desired) but as an interpreter, seeking to further mutual understanding and to maximize common ground'; 'Canada's Security in the 1980s: Options and Pitfalls' *Behind the Headlines* (pamphlet series, Canadian Institute of International Affairs) XLI 1 (1983) 12.
52 Cf Dewitt and Kirton *Canada as a Principal Power* 81–2.
53 See William R. Willoughby *The Joint Organizations of Canada and the United States* (Toronto 1979). The fourteen 'more important' binational institutions that Willoughby examines do not breach the principle of keeping supranational binational institutions to a minimum. Equal Canadian and American membership, lack of power to make binding decisions, and focus on technical and

171

relatively unpolitical issues taken together give assurance that Canadians have not surrendered veto power. If anything, they strengthen the hand of Canada's national civilian leadership. In the absence of the binational monitoring bodies decision processes might operate through professional (including military) decision structures in which Canadians might be outnumbered or dependent on Americans for essential information.

54 For example, the PJBD at no point considered questions raised about the nuclear tests at Amchitka (ibid 110). As a special-purpose instrument rather than a maid of all work it seems not to have been used as a way of dealing with 'hot' topics.

55 The Ogdensburg declaration referred to the 'defense of the north half of the Western Hemisphere,' but the PJBD's attention has in practice been focused only on the north half of that north half, i.e. the joint planning for the defense of Canada and approaches to North America along the northward great circle routes. For its specialized role in the Second World War, see Stanley W. Dziuban *Military Relations between the United States and Canada, 1939–45* (Washington, DC, 1959) chapter 2 (31–54).

56 See the two-part article by Roger F. Swanson 'The United States–Canadiana Constellation' I *International Journal* XXVII (spring 1972) 185–218, and ibid II, in XXVIII (spring 1973) 325–67; also his 'An Analytical Assessment of the United States–Canadian Defense Issue Area' in Fox, Hero, and Nye *Canada and the United States: Transnational and Transgovernmental Relations,* and Douglas J. Murray 'U.S.-Canadian Defense Relations: An Assessment for the 1980s' in Armstrong et al *Canada and the United States: Dependence and Divergence* 221–60.

57 See John W. Holmes 'The Dumbbell Won't Do' *Foreign Policy* L (spring 1983) 3–22.

CHAPTER 6: PRUDENCE, MORALITY, AND THE RANGE OF NORTH
AMERICAN CHOICE

1 Letter from George M. Wrong to Prime Minister Sir Wilfrid Laurier, 23 March 1909, quoted in Joseph Levitt *A Vision beyond Reach: A Century of Images of Canadian Destiny* 49, from Public Archives of Canada 567, Laurier Papers, 153915

2 J. Bartlet Brebner *Canada: A Modern History* (Ann Arbor, Mich, 1960) 370

3 It did not mean that Canadian interests would be protected at the expense of good relations with the United States. Thus, the British did not follow Canadian suggestions that in Anglo-American diplomacy over the building of the Panama Canal the British might try to extract some concession in the matter of the Alaskan-Canadian boundary.

4 American perceptions of Canadian 'disloyalty' and Canadian perceptions of American 'arrogance,' perhaps arising out of perceptions of a relationship that is more unequal in extra– than in intra–North American affairs, may complicate the conduct of North American affairs. For some of the complications arising even during the Cold War, when the two countries' policies were more parallel than later, see John W. Holmes 'Canada and the United States in World Politics' *Foreign Affairs* XI 1 (October 1961) especially 105–6.

5 Charles P. Stacey *Canada and the Age of Conflict* II *1921–48* (Toronto 1948) 189

6 *Theory of International Politics* (Reading, Mass, and Don Mills, Ont, 1979)

7 Though less unequal in the mid-1940s than are the United States and Canada four decades later, the United States and Britain provide an interesting parallel. Then, as in the 1980s, in a two-sided world two consequential powers on one side behaved in their relations with each other in a way that abstract theorizing about a world of the Big Two, of the Big Three, or of the Big Five does not illuminate. For an account of my own confusion in 1944 as to how many super-powers there were in a two-sided world and whether it was the number of sides or the number of super-powers or the asymmetry of organization on the two sides that was critical to understanding the post–Second World War international order, see William T.R. Fox 'The Super-Powers Then and Now' *International Journal* XXXV 3 (summer 1980) 417–36, a retrospective comment on my book *The Super-Powers* (New York 1944).

8 Arnold Wolfers *Britain and France between Two Wars* (New York 1940) emphasized that Britain and France were called upon to uphold an international order made with American – he might better have said North American – support but were left to enforce that order without its support. Canada in the League of Nations was no

more a supporter of the Versailles order than the United States out of it.

9 The new prime minister's call for 'a fresh look at the fundamentals of Canadian foreign policy' led after two years of reassessment of foreign and defense policies to the publication by the Department of External Affairs of six booklets collectively titled *Foreign Policy for Canadians* (Ottawa 1970). See Bruce Thordarson *Trudeau and Foreign Policy* (Toronto 1972) for an assessment of the assessment.

10 Charles Doran has speculated that as the Americans went through the process of 'getting back to normal size' they complicated the Canadian effort to do so. He has suggested that the relative weakening of the United States in the 1960s and 1970s both put new burdens on Canada and created new opportunities for Canada 'to translate some of its own ideals into international practice,' especially in Africa and in its mediatory role between the United States and restive European NATO partners; 'Change, Uncertainty, and Balance: A Dynamic View of United States Foreign Policy' *International Journal* XXXV 3 (summer 1980) 563–79.

11 Hughes's scornful rejoinder to the statement of the Canadian prime minister, Arthur Meighen, discussed in chapter 3, regarding Canada and the renewal of the Anglo-Japanese alliance at the conference of prime ministers, 29 June 1921, is quoted at length in Stacey *Canada and the Age of Conflict* I *1867–1921* (Toronto 1977) 342–3.

12 Thordarson (*Trudeau* 2) declared about the hearings, discussions, and debates leading to the 1970 publication of *Foreign Policy for Canadians* 'it is unlikely that any government in any country has ever subjected its external relations to such scrutiny.'

13 Notre Dame University address, 16 May 1982

14 See the annual series, *The Military Balance,* published by the International Institute of Strategic Studies (London).

15 See, for example, Annette Baker Fox 'Domestic Pressures in North America to Withdraw Forces from Europe' in William T.R. Fox and Warner R. Schilling eds *European Security and Atlantic System* (New York 1973) 197–238.

16 W.T. Stead had argued at the turn of the century that Britons had to choose between supersession by the United States in world leadership with Britain's reduction in status to that of America's Belgium and entry into 'a United States of the English-speaking World'; *The Americanization of the World* (London 1902) 151. So far

as 'America's Belgium' is concerned, British makers of foreign policy would no doubt have been glad to have Americans and Canadians believe that their own security depended on the security of the British Isles.

17 This is the issue made a matter of widespread public debate by the publication of McGeorge Bundy, Gerald Smith, Robert McNamara, and George Kennan, 'Nuclear Weapons and the Atlantic Alliance' *Foreign Affairs* LX 4 (spring 1982) 753–68.

18 Statement made at the Second United Nations General Assembly Special Session on Disarmament, 18 June 1982

19 See Charles J. Hitch and Roland McKean *The Economics of Defense in the Nuclear Age* (Cambridge, Mass, 1960), especially 3–108, on the general subject of the economics of national security.

20 Writing in a much broader international affairs context than that of 'the economics of national security,' John Holmes described Canadians as searching for 'the best mix of prosperity and interdependence obtainable, and as free a hand in policy as a middle power could expect'; *The Shaping of Peace: Canada and the Search for World Order, 1943–1957* 1 (Toronto 1979) 192.

21 See Ralph Davis *The Rise of the Atlantic Economies* (Ithaca, NY, 1973).

22 On the Canadian response to Jews fleeing Hitler see Irving M. Abella and Harold Troper *None Is Too Many: Canada and the Jews of Europe, 1933–48* (Toronto 1982).

23 Two introductions to the morally perplexing task of reconciling the claims of historic entitlement and of international distributive justice are to be found in the rigorously reasoned book by Charles R. Beitz, *Political Theory and International Relations* (Princeton, NJ, 1979), and the more policy-oriented study by Stanley Hoffmann, *Duties beyond Borders* (Syracuse, NY, 1981).

24 James Eayrs *In Defence of Canada* 1 *From the Great War to the Great Depression* (Toronto 1964) 6

25 See Harold and Margaret Sprout 'The Dilemma of Rising Demands and Insufficient Resources' *World Politics* XX 4 (July 1968) 660ff for a discussion of constraints on British foreign policy imposed by rising social demands.

26 Franz Schurmann *The Logic of World Power* (New York 1974) chapter 1. What Schurmann called American imperialism Charles Beard a generation earlier had described as a sense of world mission.

John Holmes reports that, at Bretton Woods, the 'New Dealers' had the 'itch to run the show in everybody's interest ... [and] felt they had the power and competence to manage the world for its own good because the American interest coincided with that of mankind'; *The Shaping of Peace* I 54–5.

27 Quoted in Robin Edmonds *Soviet Foreign Policy, 1962–73: The Paradox of Super-Power* (London 1975) 4, from *Istoriye Vneshei Politiki* SSR II (Moscow 1971) 480

28 J.K. Spicer *A Samaritan State? External Aid in Canada's Foreign Policy* (Toronto 1966). A more recent discussion may be found in Peyton V. Lyon and Brian W. Tomlin *Canada as an International Actor* (Toronto 1979) 140ff.

29 See R.B. Byers, Margaret MacMillan, Jacques Rastoul, Robert Spencer, and Gerald Wright *Canada and Western Security* (Toronto 1982) especially 28–37. The five authors, from five of Canada's most interested and informed organizations concerned with foreign affairs, call for both more defense effort and a more selective emphasis in choosing military roles in Western defense.

30 'What it can do best' and what other countries most need are very different criteria for applying the functional principle. Maintaining a Canadian-based air-sea transportable (CAST) group dedicated for use if needed in NATO's ACE Mobile Force in Norway presumably reflects Canada's superior ability to operate in cold climates, but the authors of *Canada and Western Security* express skepticism as to whether this ought to be a high-priority defense effort on grounds that it is not being done well and that it makes a doubtful contribution to Canadian and Western security. Nils Ørvik *Northern Development: Northern Security* (Kingston 1983) stresses the importance of Canadian forces in Europe as a political deterrent and therefore gives a lower priority to the CAST group than to the brigade in NATO's Central Command in Europe.

31 Policies can sometimes be neither prudential nor exemplary. John Sloan Dickey writes of 'the parochial mismanagement' of the energy crisis by the two North American countries; *Canada and the American Presence: The U.S. Interest in an Independent Canada* (New York 1975) 153. Rajni Kothari *Footsteps for the Future* (New York 1975) refers to the West's 'consumerism.' The compulsive focus in the energy crises of the 1970s on keeping American and Canadian cars on the road and homes at almost normal temperatures was at

the expense of both Third World energy needs and First World energy security. On the failure to take proper precautions with respect to Europe's energy security see especially David A. Deese and Joseph S. Nye eds *Energy and Security* (Cambridge, Mass, 1981).

32 Both the Wilson and Roosevelt statements are quoted in Albert K. Weinberg *Manifest Destiny: A Study of Nationalist Expansionism in American History* (Baltimore 1935) 462 and 465. As Weinberg pointed out, one reason for the fading away of 'manifest destiny' was that it got in the way of world leadership.

33 Holmes *Shaping of Peace* I 52–60

34 On 'redemptive activism' see the review article by Lewis A. Dunn, 'Past as Prologue: Redemptive Activism and the Developing World' *World Politics* XXVII 4 (July 1975) 612–27.

35 See Lyon and Tomlin *Canada as an International Actor* chapter 8, for a critical view of how the opportunity has been seized.

36 John Sloan Dickey's *Canada and the American Presence* is useful in demonstrating how an independent Canada in which policy-makers make independent calculations of what is prudent and possible and what is morally required can both by example and by friendly criticism promote the essential foreign policy objectives shared by enlightened leaders of both countries. See especially chapters 8 and 9.

Index

(1958) 92, 166; Foreign Investment Review Agency (FIRA) 93;
as high-priority foreign-policy
goal 96; vis-à-vis Britain: *see*
Imperial defense schemes; *see
also* Parallel action

Bennett, R.B. 20, 48, 100
Berger, Carl 68, 71
Bismarck, Otto von 40
Bissell, Claude T. 59, 162 n 35
Boorstin, Daniel J. 95
Borden, Sir Robert 47, 48, 50
border incidents: Confederate raid
on St Alban's, Vermont
(1864) 37; Fenian raids 38
boundary, Canada-U.S.: in Paris
peace negotiations (1782) 30;
Oregon controversy settled
(1846) 41; an 'old' boun-
dary 72–4; Alaskan-Canadian
boundary dispute 72, 164 n 4;
Point Roberts 72; in 'exclusive
economic zones' 162 n 34
Bradley, General Omar 104
Brebner, J. Bartlet 38, 58, 150–1
n 14
Britain and eighteenth-century
North America 18–19, 22–30;
colonies, king, and Parliament 19; short life of first
British North America
(1763–83) 22–3, 27; proposals
for colonial representation in
Parliament and for separate
American kingdom 26, 28;
capture of Louisbourg and
exchange for Madras 26; western lands and colonial grievan-
ces 27–30; Quebec Act
(1774) 28–9
British North America, nineteenth
century: indifference to
expected evolution toward
independence 35, 42; annexation threat as spur to Confederation 39; British North
America Act (1867) 39, 42;
failure to protect by creating
North American regional balance of power 41; Durham
report (1840) 41; recall of British garrisons 42–3, 157 n 5
Brown, Edmund G., Jr 10
Bryce, James (Lord) 113
Brezhnev, Leonid 126

Canada: as middle power 4–5;
'tyranny of proximity' to U.S. 5;
in Pacific–East Asia theater of
world politics 8; as privileged
sanctuary 13, 120–1; and
Anglo-Japanese alliance 44,
50; and foreign policy of the
British Empire 50; freedom of
foreign-policy choice 50–2, 99,
145; North American-ness
of 61–4; autonomy as priority
goal of 96; status sensitivity
of 99–100, 111; initiatives
taken before U.S. is ready to
act 107; methods of avoiding
direct confrontations with
U.S. 108; as alternate producer

of North American–type goods and services 109; as exemplar of 'North American' values 109; threats to cohesiveness of 109; as 'loyal opposition' in making policy for North America 121, and examples: Pierre Trudeau's Notre Dame University speech (1982) 106, and Lester Pearson's Temple University speech (1965) 107, 122; vulnerable location 121; *see also* Canada–U.S. relationship, French-speaking North America, Functional principle in conduct of Canadian foreign affairs, 'Third options'

Canada–United States relationship: chill and thaw in (1981–4) xiii, 80–1; unequal power in 5, 85; de facto security union 13, 104–20; travel 'along parallel roads' 59; atypicality among grossly unequal neighboring states 68–9; 'disparate dyad' relationships 69, 153 n 13; role of coercive power in 70; mutual forbearance in 90–4; Canadian sensitivity to American insensitivity 94; slow U.S. response to Canada's status sensitivities 101–2; informal access and full consultation 103, 106; economic diplomacy in 113–14; Charles Doran on asserted demise of

special relationship 164 n 4; Peyton Lyon on special characteristics of 164 n 6; *see also* Integration of U.S. and Canada, Non-linkage in Canadian-American relations, Peace in North America, Security of North America

Cancun conference (1981) 109
Canning, George 40
Chamberlain, Joseph 46
Chesterton, G.K. 33
Christie, Loring 50
collective defense and collective security 118–19; Article 51 170 n 39; *see also* North Atlantic Treaty Organization (NATO), Security in North America
Continental Congress 29
Contractual Agreement 108
Coolidge, Calvin 127

Dafoe, John W. 47–8
Declaration of Independence 29
Dehio, Ludwig 18, 29, 153
Deutsch, Karl 63
Diefenbaker, John 64
Diefenbaker-Eisenhower agreement (1958) 92
domestic affairs as challenge to primacy of foreign affairs: 'our domestic situation first' (Mackenzie King) 115; constraints on defense budget 116–17, 125; conscription issue 121; social demands vs claims of world citizenship 130–2; 141–2; *see*

181

182

Mackinder, Sir Halford: World
Island and separated North
America 6; Eurocentric geo-
politics 7; land power vs sea
power 54
Manifest Destiny 36
Marcy-Elgin treaty of trade reci-
procity (1854) 37, 155
Massey, Charles Vincent 59
Meighen, Arthur 50
'mental maps' of North
America 6–9
Monroe Doctrine, Canada
and 13, 15, 40, 114
Morgenthau, Hans 96
Mulroney, Brian xiii, 80–1

National Energy Program 85, 93,
165, 167
'Nixon shock' 164
non-events in North American
history 33
non-linkage in Canadian-
American relations 90–3, 145
North America: geopolitical vs
geographic North America 3–4,
9; separateness from Europe 6,
59, 62; facing Old World across
three oceans 7; of the Two,
Three or One? 8–12; 'southwestern' visual image of 10; as
second or 'fresh-start'
Europe 21–2, 24; as 'asylum
for mankind' 24, 128; insularity and its loss 53–4; North
Americans: how different from
whom? 57–8; North Ameri-
cans' opportunity to be virtu-

ous 58, 61–2; moral certitude
of politicians and crusade men-
tality 65–7; as 'fortunate continent' 128; as zone of peace: see
Peace in North America; see
also Europe and North America, Historic entitlement, Integration of U.S. and Canada,
Power in North America,
Security in North America
North American Accord, Reagan
proposal for (1979) 11
North American age in world
politics 118–20
North American Air Defense
Command (NORAD) 110
North American political order:
nineteenth-century 'equilibrium
of weakness' 34; stable imbalance 34, 40, 42, 52–3, 81, 91,
146; no feasible alternative
constitutional arrange-
ments 82–3; non-state actors
and balancing process 86–9;
satisfactions for Canada in
existing order 94; North American 'civic order' 103; Pierre
Trudeau on Canada's looking-
glass function 106, 148; Lester
Pearson's Temple University
speech (1965) 107, 122; Canada's burden in maintain-
ing 111; Canada as 'loyal
opposition' 121; see also
Canada-U.S. relationship, Parallel action, Peace in North
America
North Atlantic Treaty and North

response 12–13; unneutral neutrality in Second World War 19; disunited states of Europe as godparents of 29; as world's 'first new nation' 39, 62; separation of powers and U.S. foreign affairs 62; 'bad-neighbor' environment policies 91; 'hyperopia' in conduct of foreign relations 94; 'global isolationism' and sense of world mission 96, 133, 138, 141–2; anti-colonialism and informal imperialism 114; asserted decline in power of 119–20; *see also* Ogdensburg declaration
United States–Canada relationship: *see* Canada–United States relationship

Vereeniging, Peace of (1902) 47
Versailles, treaty of (1919) 48
Vietnam war 119
Viner, Jacob 165

Waltz, Kenneth N. 117
War of 1812 31–3
Washington Conference on Naval Disarmament 50–1
Washington, treaty of (1871): *see* Anglo-Atlantic system
Whitman, Walt 59
Wilson, Woodrow 58, 138
Wrong, George M. 112
Wrong, Hume 61